Torpedoed!

Surviving the Lusitania

Torpedoed!
Surviving the Lusitania

David Dubczak

Conjunction Media

To Laura

And to all those with imagination.

Chapter 1

May 1, 1915

Crowds overflowed the docks on New York City's "Ocean Liner Row." People of all kinds mixed together among rows and rows of giant steel ocean liners. Some people coming to

America, and some people leaving. Some rich people, and many more poor people. Some people loading the magnificent vessels with cargo, and some unloading.

And then some, like Leo Masterson and his friend George, ran through the crowd. The shadows of the massive steel ships towered above them. They bumped into ladies who were dressed in their best, and gentlemen wearing top hats.

This is New York. Even on the piers, everyone is always busy.

"C'mon, George!" Leo shouted back at his friend. "The Lusitania leaves at ten!"

"I'm not sure we should be doing this!" George shouted back. He waved a newspaper page in Leo's direction. "The Germans say they'll sink her!"

Leo stopped, and rubbed the sweat out of his blonde hair. "They'll have to catch her first," he said, "And *nothing* can catch the Lusitania." Leo pointed behind him, "Lusitania can go faster than any ship in the ocean, and any torpedo."

George followed Leo's finger and looked behind him. He jumped! This ship was far bigger than the ship he and Leo had just left. Far bigger than he had imagined!

He heard of the *Titanic*, the famous ship that sank three years earlier. Titanic was supposed to be unsinkable, but she sank on her very first voyage! George couldn't imagine any ship being bigger than the giant Lusitania that floated in front of him. Pier 54 was Lusitania's home in New York. All of Pier 54 was in the shadow of Lusitania's long hull and four giant black smokestacks.

"It's plenty safe," Leo said again. "Besides, do you want to be stuck on a slow cargo boat going to Australia for who knows how long? Lusitania will have us home next week."

Home, George thought. *Home sounds nice*. He thought of his mother's cozy house in Liverpool, England. Both Leo and George needed jobs, and Leo got them a job on a cargo ship sailing from England, to New York, to Australia. That slow ship would take six months to make the journey.

But now, Leo had a better idea. They would abandon their cargo ship and get hired to work on the Lusitania.

Leo could see George was nervous. He turned around and walked under the giant sign that said the name of Lusitania's owner: CUNARD. If George didn't want to join him, he would go alone.

Chapter 2

Cunard's Pier 54 was over eight hundred feet long, slightly longer than the Lusitania. Ramps from the pier floor rested against the side of the ship. Passengers and Crew moved up and down the ramps from the pier to the ship.

Leo and George found a giant sign labeled CREW. They ran to it, and the man at the desk just stared at them. "Go away, kids," the man said in a British accent. "I'm trying to hire a crew for Lusitania."

"I'm seventeen," Leo replied. "And I have my Mate's License." He pointed to George. "And this is my friend George. We both came to New York as crew members of the SS Carola."

The man eyed them suspiciously. "This is a British ship, and the law says it must have a British crew. Are you British?"

"Absolutely, sir," Leo said.

"God Save the King," George answered.

The man kept looking at them suspiciously. "Why aren't you fighting in the war?" he asked.

Leo and George looked at each other. What could they say? They didn't *want* to fight in the war. They went out to sea to stay away from it. But, the endlessly long crossing on the SS Carola made them homesick. They couldn't imagine sailing on the rusty, stinky Carola for another six months.

Finally, Leo shrugged and said, "Someone has to crew the ships."

"I'll say, you're right about that," the man told them. "I can't hardly find enough crew for Cunard's ships. All the British men are off fighting the war! It's so bad, they canceled *Camaronia's* sailing, and all her passengers and crew are coming over to Lusitania."

The man reached under his desk, then handed them clipboards with some papers to fill out. "How do they expect me to find a British crew in New York? Alright, I'll bring you aboard," he said. "Leo, you'll be an Able-Bodied Seaman, and George, you'll be a Trimmer."

They smiled as they filled out their forms. They both knew those jobs, jobs they did on the Carola. Leo knew how to work on the deck, cleaning, fixing, pulling ropes. He could handle anything that needed to be done! His hard-earned experience might make him one of the most useful crewmen on the ship.

George was a trimmer on the Carola, and now he would be one on the Lusitania. Burning coal powered Lusitania's engines. On her way to England, she would burn thousands of tons of coal. The coal was stored in big rooms they called "bunkers" that ran along the side of the ship. George would help keep the weight of the coal spread out evenly so the ship wouldn't lean to one side, or "list" as the sailors said.

"You better get aboard," the man hurried them. "She leaves at ten."

Leo and George finished their paperwork and then rushed up the crew ramp into the Lusitania, to join the other 694 crew, and 1,294 passengers. A full ship.

But Lusitania would not leave at ten. Transferring the passengers and crew from the Camaronia took longer than expected, and they didn't leave until after noon.

They didn't know it yet, but that was just enough of a delay to put them directly into harm's way. Looking up at the portholes along Lusitania's side reminded him that being in harm's way was something Leo already knew too much about.

Chapter 3

Five Years Ago

Twelve-year-old Leo stood on the bow at the very front of the rickety old fishing steamer off the coast of England. The single smokestack chugged angry black soot as the rusty iron hulk limped through the choppy water.

The elderly captain stood at the helm steering the ship from the open-air bridge of the 100-foot ship. His name was Bartholamew or Barty or Barry or something like that. He seemed too old to talk, and only captained the SS Rusticle because his fingers had grown permanently wrapped around the helm.

A crew of boys who lied about their age, just like Leo, stood ready to pull up nets full of fish and take them back into Liverpool. He could pass for fifteen, and it was good enough to get him the job.

But he didn't know what he was doing. Leo didn't know that the "bow" was the front and the "stern" was the back. He didn't know that the "helm" was the steering wheel, and that the "bridge" was where the captain commanded the ship. He didn't know any of the dozens of types of rope knots sailors were required to know. He didn't know that, if you faced the front, the right side was "starboard" and the left was "port."

And, he didn't know how to swim. But that didn't bother the grayed, wrinkly, old captain. "If we sink," the captain told him, "knowing how to swim just prolongs your suffering."

Leo needed the job, and he would learn anything he needed to. He wished he could be at the helm with the captain, but it seemed like all he needed to know was how to pull nets full of fish out of the ocean.

The crew of five boys, just like him, stayed in bunks in a room below decks. At night, they slept with their porthole open. Otherwise, the air inside became stuffy and miserable. If their miserable rust-pile of a vessel had a name on its bow, it was hidden under years of peeling paint and disintegrating steel.

Suddenly, while waiting to pull up the nets, the deck under Leo's feet bounced, and he heard a loud, dull rumble coming from deep within. He looked up at the smokestack in the middle. The smoke seemed different - dirtier, grittier... angrier.

Then, an explosion! A hole blew out in the port side below the water, and steam erupted through the sea. The inexperienced crew running the ancient steam engine below decks had built up too much steam pressure, and the steam burst out of the engine and punched a big hole in the port side!

The rust bucket was going down. As cold sea water filled in the hole, it hit the hot boilers and instantly burst into steam, causing more ruptures in the deck and hull.

It sounded to Leo like his ship was being eaten and sucked down by an angry, hungry sea dragon! The ship tossed and turned, the rushing water constantly changing the ship's balance.

"Make a jump for it!" the captain called from the bridge. "She's gonna blow up!"

Leo couldn't swim, and neither could anyone else! A crate on the deck held some life jackets, and they all rushed to grab them. But the jackets were old, never used, torn, and weathered. They didn't know if the life jackets would work, but they quickly threw them over their heads and tied them on.

Then, without thinking, Leo ran over to the starboard railing and hurled himself over!

Suddenly, Leo found himself back inside the ship! He lay on his back, the bunk room filling with water. The ship had sunk low enough that the porthole reached the water, and the water rushing through sucked Leo back inside!

Grunting and screaming, he pushed himself back to the window and tried to climb out, but it didn't work! Every time he pushed himself halfway through the window, the rushing water pushed him back in!

The bunk room quickly filled with water. He pushed himself to the door, but the violent tossing and turning had bent the door frame, and the door wouldn't open. He was trapped!

There wasn't time to scream for help. The hole in the ship's port side was too big and the ship was too small. Anyone who could help him was already in the water.

Within seconds, he took his final breath as the last bit of air escaped out of the room. He held his breath under water, when he noticed a new feeling: water had stopped rushing in. It was still. No more water flowed in once the room was full.

This may be the last thing he ever did, but he pushed his feet against the wall behind him and aimed toward the open porthole. This time, he made it all the way through, and his life jacket floated him to the water's surface.

They all nearly died because the crew didn't know what they were doing. The engine man didn't know it was close to exploding. Once it had, Leo and the rest of the inexperienced boys didn't know how to save themselves.

Leo determined, while floating off the English coast, he would never again be one of those people. He would learn to swim. He would learn the ways of the sea and become the best sailor in all of England.

Chapter 4

May 1, 1915

Leo walked the boat deck, the very top deck of the ship. Under the morning sun, he wore his new flat hat and blue crewman's uniform. His first job was to meet his bunkmate, Clyde Prescott, a boy about the same age as him and another able-bodied seaman.

Leo and Clyde were the same age, but Clyde seemed older. He spoke more gruff, and he moved slower, almost angry. Leo and Clyde were instructed to scrub the decks together.

"Put yer back into it," Clyde huffed at Leo. But Leo *was* putting his back into it. He dipped the brush on the end of his pole into the bucket of soapy water, and then leaned into it as he scraped all the dirt off the deck.

But Leo scoffed. He didn't like being told how to do things he already knew how to do. "I know how to scrub a deck, mate, thank you," he said. He knew so much more than just how to scrub decks. He should be bossing Clyde around!

"Coal dust sticks into this wood," Clyde told him with a gravely voice. "You got to keep it out, or Captain Turner'll be mad!" Then, Clyde stopped mopping and grabbed Leo by his loose sailor's tie. "Captain Turner's tough. He means business. You gotta work hard, or he'll fire you and you'll wind up fighting in the war."

The war.

Leo didn't want to be in the war. It seemed like all of Europe was at war against each other. Before joining his last ship, he read all about the war in the newspapers.

Before the war, all the countries in Europe had agreements to defend each other. Leo remembered the word "ally." When two countries were friends, they were "allies."

It all started with Archduke Ferdinand. He was the nephew of the Emperor of Austria-Hungary. When Serbian criminals killed Archduke Ferdinand, Austria-Hungary declared war on Serbia.

Then, Serbia's ally Russia declared war on Austria-Hungary. Then Austria's ally Germany declared war on Russia. France was Russia's ally, so Germany declared war on them, too. So then, France's ally England declared war on Germany.

And now, all of Europe was at war against each other. All because the Emperor's nephew was killed. People back home called it "The Great War." Leo thought it was the stupidist war ever.

Leo wanted to be at sea, away from it all. If he could stay on the Lusitania, he would sail back and forth from England to New York and be able to visit home every two weeks, without having to fight in the war.

Leo and Clyde continued to brush along the wooden deck as passengers explored about. "The Germans want to sink this ship, ya know," it seemed like Clyde was trying to scare him. "That's why the old captain left."

"The old captain?" Leo asked, as he kept brushing.

"Yeah," Clyde explained. "Captain Dow. He asked to be moved off Lusitania because he didn't have the nerve to sail a passenger liner through a war zone anymore."

Clyde stopped brushing and looked out, past the deck, toward England. "When we get to England, there'll be German submarines with torpedoes all over the place."

Leo smiled, and just kept brushing. "Lusitania's too fast to get hit with a torpedo. If we see one coming, we'll just turn and steam away. That's why I got on this boat."

"We'll see about that," Clyde snarked.

As Leo brushed, he spied another able-bodied seaman that looked to be struggling with some rope. Leo stopped brushing for a moment to see. It looked like the rope had broken, and the stack of deck chairs he was trying to tie down had fallen all over the place!

Leo and Clyde ran over to help.

"Yer rope's broken!" Clyde shouted.

"Yeah, sorry," the sailor sheepishly replied. "It got caught on something and cut part way through."

Clyde put his hands on his hips. "Yer gonna have to go get a new rope and clean up this mess," he ordered, as if Lusitania was *his* ship.

"Wait!" Leo interrupted before the sailor could move. "I have an idea. Do you know how to do a *sheet bend?*"

The sailor shook his head to say 'no.' Leo took the two broken ends of the rope, and held one end in a U shape. He passed the other end through the U, and tied it off around the top half of the U. "This is a knot called a *sheet bend*," he explained. "You can use it to tie two lines together. A lot of knots come apart when the rope isn't tight, but not a sheet bend."

The sailor looked astonished! "Gee, thanks!" he exclaimed.

"Quite welcome," Leo answered, and then left the sailor to go back to his mop. An angry Clyde followed, disgruntled to be shown up in front of people.

Clyde said nothing to Leo as they continued to scrub the deck of the persistent coal soot. They made no sound except for the soft back and forth brushing of bristles working the coal soot out of the wood.

As Leo brushed, he looked at the long ramps connecting Lusitania to the pier, and the passengers still boarding the ship. Almost directly below him, the first class gangway rested against the ship. He watched for a moment as men in top hats and women in glorious, colorful, puffy gowns strolled up the gangway. The war in Europe didn't exist here in New York, and the passengers boarded for just another trip.

Then, from the corner of his eye, he spied someone. Someone familiar! Could it be?

A girl walked up the gangway dressed in the fluffy black and white maid's outfit. She followed a woman up the ramp, holding her bags. Her blonde hair was tied up under a small bonnet.

It was Leo's sister, Martha! Martha served as a maid to Mrs. Elizabeth Beauclerk, the wealthy wife of a banker in London. The last Leo heard, Mr. Beauclerk sent his wife and her maid to New York at the outbreak of the war. He didn't know why they would be headed home, but here they were!

Leo propped his broom against a lifeboat. "I'll be right back," he shouted back to Clyde.

As Clyde watched Leo run off down the deck, he looked around to make sure no one was watching him. Then, he dumped over Leo's dirty bucket of water all over the deck Leo had just cleaned.

"Oops," Clyde said with a mean smile. Then he gathered his equipment and moved to another section of the deck.

Chapter 5

Mrs. Beauclerk and Martha stepped off the gangway onto the enclosed promenade deck. Leo ran down a single flight of stairs and spotted them about to enter the Main Staircase on B Deck. "Martha!" he shouted in a way that was inappropriate for a crew member to shout. "Martha!" he shouted again. His voice echoed off the steel ceiling.

Martha trailed behind Mrs. Beauclerk, and continued to stare straight forward, as if she thought she was only imagining hearing her name called.

"Martha!" Leo called one more time, running closer, and getting irritated looks from the wealthy passengers he passed.

Finally, Martha looked, and the surprise Leo saw in her face radiated true joy. "Leo!" she called out, dropping her bags and running toward him. Martha jumped into Leo's arms with a giant hug.

"Leo, what are you doing here?" Martha asked.

"I just joined the crew! What are you doing here?"

Martha looked back at her boss. "Mrs. Beauclerk said we needed to go home."

Mrs. Beauclerk, unlike the rest of the first class passengers, was not dressed in her best. She wore a simple blue blouse and yellow skirt, with no hat to cover her long red hair. She joined them, and looked quizzically at Martha.

"Mrs. Beauclerk, this is my brother, Leo," she explained. "He's a crewman here on the Lusitania."

But Mrs. Beauclerk just stared past him, hardly acknowledging his presence. "The spirits are baffling me these days," she said, with a low, ominous voice. "First, they told me to go home. But then, when we arrived in New York, they give me only visions of death! I tried to miss this sailing, but now that it's after ten and the ship's still here, I might as well get aboard."

Martha looked at Leo and just shrugged. Mrs. Beauclerk is like this all the time, it seems.

A new voice startled Leo. "Excuse me!" a sharp voice ordered. Leo turned around to see a tall, perfectly-dressed officer looking directly at him.

The officer approached. From the stripes on his uniform, Leo figured him to be either the ship's second or third officer. "You're not allowed to talk to the passengers," the officer told him, and then turned to Mrs. Beauclerk. "My apologies, madam."

Mrs. Beauclerk lightened up, as if the weight of the "spirits" had just left. She smiled at the officer. "Oh, sir," she said, "Don't worry. I called him over to speak with us!"

The officer looked again at Leo. From behind him, Leo saw Mrs. Beauclerk wink! This answer was clearly not what the officer wanted.

"Indeed," the officer said. "And when you're all finished catching up, sailor, I expect you'll return to your post?"

Leo nodded. "I will, sir."

The officer stood straight, and left, going about his business of preparing the ship for departure.

"Thank you!" Leo gasped, grateful for her kindness.

"Martha's told me a lot about you, Leo," Mrs. Beauclerk replied. "And Martha, we should find our cabin. This dark voyage has me tired already."

Martha and Leo hugged one more time. "We'll see each other around, Leo?" she asked.

Leo smiled. "It's a big ship, but it's only a ship."

Then, Martha smiled and waved goodbye, as she followed Mrs. Beauclerk inside.

Maybe, when they got to Liverpool, they would be able to see their mother together. Perhaps they could use the wireless radio to send their mother a message to meet them at the docks.

Leo smiled, happy with his decision to join the Lusitania's crew. This would be a great voyage.

Chapter 6

With a deafening bellow of the ship's steam whistle on the top of her first funnel, Lusitania finally departed New York. Leo watched a small team of tugboats expertly push and pull the giant liner out of its slip and turn it down the Hudson River toward the Atlantic Ocean. Once the ship cast off its ropes, Leo worked a rope near the bow. Being at the front of the ship gave him a great view of the majestic buildings the Lusitania passed on each side.

As he coiled up the heavy rope, he felt a tap on his shoulder. He turned around. It was Martha, and she didn't look happy!

"What are you doing on this ship, Leo?" Martha asked with folded arms.

"What do you mean?" Leo shrugged, and kept working.

"The Germans want to sink her."

"Well, then, I should ask, what are *you* doing on this ship?" Leo smartly quipped.

"*I* don't have a choice. I have to go wherever Mrs. Beauclerk goes." Martha stared him down. "Didn't you have a job on a freighter?"

Leo kept coiling up the rope, as a team of sailors on each side worked their own ropes. "That rust bucket would have taken six months to get to Australia," he said. "This way, I get to see mom every two weeks and make sure she's all right."

"You never *think*, Leo," Martha scolded him. "You alway rush into things without thinking and that gets you in trouble."

"Martha, it's *fine*," Leo tried to reassure her. "Lusitania's too fast for a torpedo to catch her. Besides, when we get close, you think a ship this big and this important won't have a navy ship to see us safely in?"

Martha just crossed her arms and turned around, too frustrated with her brother, and knowing she wouldn't change his mind. It was too late, anyway. They were already on their way.

"Just promise me you'll *think* before you *act*, Leo," Martha demanded. "Remember that time you almost died?"

Leo didn't know what to say. He just kept coiling up his rope. "I do remember," he finally answered, "and I know a whole lot more than I did back then."

From the bow of the ship, Martha could see the front of the boat deck behind the bridge where Captain Turner and the officers commanded the ship. It looked like a small crew of sailors and an officer were gathered around a lifeboat.

"What are they doing?" Martha asked.

Leo looked. "Probably a lifeboat drill," he said. "Practicing how to get one ready to lower."

Martha looked on and studied for a few moments more. "Do you suppose they know what they're doing?" She asked Leo.

She didn't like what she saw. The men were clumsy. The officer kept pointing things out and having them redo their work. The white cranes, or davits, from which the boat hung jerked back and forth as the crew struggled to crank the boat out over the side of the ship. The blue-suited men kept running into each other, and one even fell as he tripped over his fellow crewman!

Leo didn't like what he saw either. "All of the experienced sailors are in the Navy. This is what we have left," he explained. Not that it made either of them feel better.

"You know how to lower one though, right?" Martha asked.

Leo nodded and said, "Yes." He lied.

As Leo, Martha, and the rest of the Lusitania sailed slowly through New York Harbor, they passed the *SS Vaterland*, a German passenger ship.

Though the United States is not a part of the war, the country is quietly friends with England. Germany and England are enemies. Now, the *Vaterland* sat quiet, empty, and not going anywhere. The entire crew of the *Vaterland* had been arrested. It seems the war *was* in New York.

The war was everywhere.

Chapter 7

Lusitania said deep into her first night away from New York. By the time evening fell, blackness was all around them. Leo couldn't see the city lights off the stern behind him. Only the stars overhead broke the blackness that surrounded the Lusitania and the yellow glow cast on the decks by her own lights.

Leo missed the look of Cunard's orange funnels. Every ship in Cuard's fleet sported funnels painted with the distinctive "Cunard Orange." But now, for better camouflage in the war, Lusitania's four funnels were disguised in flat black. They said it would make it blend into the water and harder for submarines to tell what ship they were looking at.

But the sound was everywhere. Black smoke and steam billowed out of the four giant funnels. The roar of the burning coal from the boilers below echoed through each funnel. On the deck, big brown vents shaped like soup cans with open lids and large enough to fit a whole person sent fresh air down to the boiler rooms. Clanging rang up the vents from the firemen down below who continuously shoveled coal into the fires.

Burning coal kept the ship moving. Moving kept the Lusitania safe.

The boat deck was a noisy place under the sound of the smoke escaping the funnels and the roar of the ship's bow slicing through the water. It was May, and it was still cold. Leo buttoned his coat a little tighter. Most of the passengers preferred to be in the enclosed promenade below them, or inside. The speed of the ship created a wind that further chilled the air atop the deck.

Leo's shift was over. He was supposed to be in bed. But he had work to do.

A special staircase took them from the crew's quarters to the boat deck, in Lusitania's midship. He whistled for George, who nervously followed him.

"We shouldn't be up here, Leo," George said, uncomfortable in his borrowed sailor's uniform. Only the able-bodied seamen, like Leo, got to wear these uniforms. For firemen and trimmers, it was black pants and a white sleeveless shirt to help them withstand the heat from the boilers down below.

"We gotta figure out how to lower one of these," Leo loudly whispered. "Not many of the crew know how."

"Haven't they been practicing?" a puzzled George asked.

"Practicing it once doesn't mean you know," Leo shot back, impatiently. "We have to *know*."

They carefully looked both ways. The deck was clear of people, but crowded with boats. After the *Titanic* disaster, every passenger ship packed their decks with as many lifeboats as they could get. Every inch of the boat deck was lined with lifeboats, and under each boat was another type of boat called a "collapsible."

The collapsibles had canvas sides that needed to be raised, but until then, fit nicely under the regular lifeboats. If they needed to be used, the crew would lower the regular lifeboat, crank the hooks back up, and hook up one of the collapsibles to be lowered.

If they knew how, and *if* they had time.

"I thought you had your mate's license?" George asked, confused and shivering. Spending all day in the heat of the boiler rooms made the chilly deck feel even worse. "Isn't this part of your training?"

"Yeah, but these are different," Leo said, studying the boat's pulleys. "I've never been on a ship like this."

George scratched his head. "Why do we have to do this now?"

Leo stepped to the side of one of the canvas-covered lifeboats. "Because there's German submarines all over that want to sink us," he snapped at George.

"But, you said Lusitania's too fast for anything to sink her?" George seemed confused.

Leo looked right at him. "That was before I knew my sister was aboard."

George was surprised at Leo's intensity. He's normally very calm, happy, and even joking. But his eyes told George that Leo is dead serious.

"All good, mate," George replied. "What do we need to do?"

Leo studied the lifeboat. On each end of the boat, a crane towered over it. The white crane they called a "davit" stood straight up, but then curved over the top of the boat. A system of ropes and pulleys connected the davit to the end of the boat. A canvas cover wrapped around the boat's top. The extra rope for the pulley system was carefully coiled under the canvas.

"I know we need to get the ropes out," Leo said. "Let's take the top off."

"Don't make too much noise," George replied, and then helped Leo with the canvas.

After they loosened the canvas, they rolled it up and set it inside the boat so it wouldn't roll anywhere or fly away in the ship's wind. They reached inside and removed the long, heavy, coiled rope, and set the extra length down next to the davits.

Behind them, through the windows of the first class writing saloon, a few curious passengers started watching through the windows. George and Leo didn't notice.

"What's next?" George asked.

"We have to swing out the davits," Leo explained. Inside the boat, he saw two long cranks. At the bottom of the davits, it looked like the crank inserted into a screw. By turning the screw, the top of the davit would swing out over the side of the ship, and the boat would hang from it.

George and Leo took the handles of the cranks and inserted it into the screws. They started turning. The top of the davits slowly rotated outwards. Then, they stopped. No matter how hard George and Leo pushed on their cranks, the davits would not move further.

"What's wrong?" asked George.

"I don't know," Leo shook his head.

The sound of the wind and the ship slicing through the water covered the footsteps of oncoming crewmen. They startled and jumped when their visitors spoke.

"That's them!"

Leo turned around. It was Clyde, with a mean look on his face. Clyde seemed to have brought an officer. It was the same junior officer that got mad at Leo for talking to Martha earlier that day.

"What are you two boys doing?" the officer sharply inquired.

George stood, stunned, unable to come up with anything to say. Leo gulped. "Um... practicing?"

"On whose orders?" the officer barked.

Again, Leo stammered. "Um, we just thought, since we, um, we didn't have..."

"They didn't have permission, that's what I *told* you!" Clyde bragged to the officer.

Leo gulped. He didn't want to be fired. He didn't want to get sent off to fight in the war. He just wanted to try to help, to do a good thing. What would this officer do?

"It takes four men to launch one of these boats," the officer said, obviously not happy. "The way you were doing it, you could have dropped it into the water."

"Then it's a good thing you were here!" A new voice caught them all by surprise. The figure was tall and imposing, with an old, experienced, full face. Leo looked at the stripes on his uniform.

It was Captain Turner.

"Mister Bisset," Turner said, "tell these boys how to do it properly."

"It's *Bestic*, sir, with all due respect," the officer told the captain. Now Leo knew this was Junior Third Officer Albert Bestic.

"*Bestic*, my apologies," replied Captain Turner. "Now, tell these boys how to do it properly."

Bestic motioned toward the ropes. "It takes four men," he explained. "Two to pull the ropes and lift the boat, and two more to swing out the davits. You were trying to drag the boat out of its mounts. If you had done that, without holding on to the ropes, it would've fallen right into the water."

George and Leo looked at each other, grateful for his explanation. Clyde, however, crossed his arms, certain they were about to be reprimanded for breaking the rules.

"Thank you!" Leo said.

George followed his lead and nodded his head profusely. "Yes, thank you, sir."

Captain Turner turned his head toward Leo. "You want to be an officer some day, son?"

Leo nodded. "Yes, sir. Yes, I do."

"Bisset, help them get the boat stowed away," the Captain ordered. "And tomorrow, see to it that they get a chance to practice rigging it properly."

Then, Turner looked back at Leo and George. "Boys," he said, "I'm grateful for your ambition. But don't alarm the passengers."

Leo and George looked and saw a small crowd gathered to watch them through the saloon windows. When they looked back, Captain Turner was gone.

Clyde seemed to be steaming more than the funnels. He glared at Leo angrily.

"Well, you heard the Captain, hurry up!" Officer Bestic ordered. He helped them secure the boat in place and replace the canvas cover.

Inside the saloon, Leo could not have known that the passengers' fascination with the lifeboat was out of fear. Every passenger was well aware: when they reached England, German submarines would be everywhere.

Chapter 8

May 3, 1915

"Masterson!"

Leo blinked his eyes. Everything was blurry.

Working on a ship is hard work. Sailors don't get time off. They work until it's their turn to sleep. Then, they wake up and get back to work. Leo worked so hard yesterday he didn't even remember going to bed.

"Masterson!"

Leo turned his head and blinked again. Third Officer Bestic stood over his bunk in the seamen's quarters.

"Masterson, get up!" Officer Bestic shouted.

"Yeah, yeah!" Leo groaned, still coming to. "Sorry. Yes, sir? What can I do, sir?"

"In Cargo Hold Number One is a trunk belonging to Mrs. Beauclerk in stateroom B-31. You are to retrieve it and deliver it to Mrs. Beauclerk."

Leo jumped out of his top bunk. The seamen's bunkroom had room for thirty, in ten bunks stacked three high. He blinked the sleep out of his eyes again. "Am I... am I late, sir?" he stammered.

Bestic shook his head. "No. Your shift is just starting. Get yourself presentable and go retrieve that trunk. She asked for you specifically."

With more work to do, Bestic turned and left. Leo looked out the porthole. With his quarters being just above the water, he could see the ocean ripping by as Lusitania plowed through the early morning sea.

After going to the shared bathroom down the hall and washing his face, brushing his hair, and putting on his blue sailor's uniform, Leo made his way down the long crew passageway forward to Cargo Hold Number One.

Clyde came running up behind him. "Leo!" he shouted. "Leo! Let me help."

Leo was not excited to see Clyde, especially after last night. "I don't need help to retrieve a trunk, Clyde," Leo said.

Clyde finally caught up to him. "I'm sorry about the other night," he apologized. "Let me lend a hand. It's the least I can do."

Leo nodded, and opened the door to the forward cargo hold. Inside, a set of steps took them almost to the very bottom of the ship.

The ship was not very wide at this point, and Leo could cross from one side to another in only a few steps. Shelves lined the walls. In the middle, he looked up and saw a canvas hatch several decks above him. When they reached Liverpool, he suspected he would be one of the crewmen who opened the hatch and used the electric crane on the top deck to hoist the bags out of the hold.

On the shelves and on the floor, large nets held everything down. The waves in the middle of the Atlantic could grow large, and storms formed from nowhere. Lusitania was built to withstand anything. The nets helped make sure, no matter what happened, the cargo wouldn't move.

Trunks, bags, and boxes of all sorts filled the hold. Leo and Clyde walked around, looking for anything labeled with Mrs. Beauclerk's name.

Finally, in a stack of bags and trunks in the middle of the floor, they saw a large purple trunk tagged with "Beauclerk, B-31."

Leo and Clyde worked together to unhook the nets that covered the entire pile. It wasn't easy. The nets were tied down tight! They grunted and groaned to untie the corners until the net finally loosened free.

Clyde pushed over a cart from the corner, and Leo hoisted the trunk onto it. "Can you get it to B-31 by yourself?" Clyde asked.

"I certainly think so," Leo said.

"Good then," Clyde replied. "I'll take care of things here."

Leo squinted. "Are you sure?" He asked. "The nets have to be tied down really tight to keep things from coming loose."

"I got it!" Clyde assured him.

Leo simply nodded, and pushed the trunk out of the hold. He needed to get it to the lifts amidships.

Once Leo was safely out of the room, Clyde went about removing every net along the wall. The next time the ship hit heavy seas, all of the bags would come tumbling down.

Clyde couldn't wait to tell an officer how sloppy Leo had handled the nets in the baggage hold, and how careless he was to leave them all loose!

Chapter 9

Leo tried not to make too much noise as he pushed the cart down the long hallway on B Deck. On a ship, they call them *corridors*, and the corridor down to B-31 was carpeted and wood-paneled with a very light-colored wood.

A few passengers sneered at him and gave him disapproving looks. A sailor of his rank was usually not allowed in First Class corridors. Retrieving a trunk was the job of a steward trained in the special art of politeness First Class passengers required.

Finally, he reached B-31, nearly at the front of the ship, on the starboard side. Gently, he knocked on the door. Martha answered, and her shocked face told Leo she did not expect to see him.

"Leo!" she exclaimed. "Why are you here? Are you supposed to be here?"

From behind her, at the back of the glamorous first class stateroom, Mrs. Beauclerk called out. "Oh, I asked for him specifically! I needed to retrieve an item from this trunk."

"Here it is, Ma'am," Leo said, pushing the trunk into the room.

Mrs. Beauclerk, who wore a fluffy yellow dress she called a *morning gown*, made her way to the trunk. "You two catch up while I dig through this thing," she said to both Leo and Martha.

For a moment, Leo and Martha stood, not sure what to say to each other. Finally, Leo said, "We practiced lowering some of the lifeboats yesterday."

"Did it go well?" Martha asked, her eyebrows raised.

"Yes, but we won't need to use them."

"Why not?"

They both answered at the same time. Martha already knew his answer. "Because Lusitania's too fast."

At that moment, Mrs. Beauclerk pulled a small book out of her trunk with such force it nearly flew into the air. "Ahh!" she lightly shrieked, then looked embarrassed. "Sorry, my dream journal."

When she could tell both Leo and Martha were confused, she explained, "I write my dreams down every day. It helps me establish patterns, to see my life more clearly." Then, her face changed. Her eyes turned dark, scared, and sad. "It seems I've had the most dreadful dreams the past two nights."

As fast as her dark mood came, it left her. She blinked and shook it off, and then returned to her delightful mood! "Young man," she said, "we require your knowledge of this vessel to escort us to the First Class lounge."

"But ma'am," Leo protested, "I only joined this vessel two days ago. I don't know it very well. It's quite large."

With a knowing glance, Mrs. Beauclerk winked at him and smiled. "Your sister tells me you love ships. I need *your* specific expertise!"

Leo looked over at Martha. He does love ships. Although he loved sailing on the crew, he wasn't allowed in many of Lusitania's best places, like the First Class lounge. It seemed Mrs. Beauclerk was doing him a favor!

"Yes, ma'am," he said, trying to hold back his smile.

"Good then," she replied. "Escort us to the lounge, and then you can return this trunk back into the cargo hold."

They left the room, and Leo led them down the long, white hallway to the First Class lounge. Mrs. Beauclerk left her dream journal on her night stand. Writing down her ghastly dreams over the Lusitania's fate would wait until later.

Chapter 10

Leo led Martha and Mrs. Beauclerk up the stairs to A Deck, the top level of the ship. Through the hallway's windows, they could see the Boat Deck lined with lifeboats.

At the top of the main staircase landing, swinging doors showed them the way to the lounge. Inside, dark wood walls supported a decorative white ceiling. In the middle of the room, a stained-glass skylight gave light to everything. Cloth-covered chairs and couches filled the rooms. The richest passengers on the ship milled about, chatting and drinking tea.

"Ah, Mrs. Beauclerk!" a voice shouted to them from across the room. "Please, do join me!" A man waved to them from across the room, and Mrs. Beauclerk smiled and headed in his direction.

"That's Alfred Vanderbilt," Martha whispered to Leo. "He's one of the richest people in the United States. His family built most of the railroads."

Leo didn't know what to say. He had never stood amongst this much money in his entire life.

"How do you do?" Mrs. Beauclerk greeted Mr. Vanderbilt.

"Oh, just fine, Lizzie," he replied. "I've made your acquaintance, but I haven't had a chance to talk to you yet. What brings you aboard?"

Mrs. Beauclerk sat down on a couch across from Vanderbilt, and Martha dutifully stood off to the side, waiting for her employer to provided instructions. Leo, not knowing what to do, stood next to her.

"Oh, it's dreadful," Mrs. Beauclerk exclaimed, "I would much rather not be on board. The spirits are shouting me warnings! But, with the war and all, this may be the last crossing to England for quite some time."

"Well, it certainly will be if the Germans sink us!" Vanderbilt laughed, and Leo found it quite odd. In fact, as Leo looked around, most of the room seemed to be laughing with him!

"What are the odds at, right now?" Vanderbilt asked.

An older man, dressed in a casual suit for the morning, shouted from across the room. "Ten to one, good fellow!" A few more men chuckled.

Ten to one? Leo thought. What did that mean?

"Blimey!" Mrs. Beauclerk exclaimed. "Are you men placing *bets* on our fate?"

Mr. Vanderbilt smiled and laughed again. "Well, Lizzie, we have to have some good fun among all our worry!"

Ten to one. Now Leo understood. For every one person who bet the ship would arrive safely, ten thought it would be sunk by a German torpedo.

"And how would those who bet against us presume to collect?" Mrs. Beauclerk asked, sternly. "I've never seen such a *stupid* voyage."

"Now, now, Lizzie," Vanderbilt shook his head. "It's all good fun. Of course we'll have a navy escort when we reach English waters. There's nothing to worry about."

The room's attention turned to an officer entering from the outside. "Morning, ladies and gents," the officer greeted the room.

Leo recognized him from passing. It was Chief Steward John Jones. He was the head of all the stewards, and in charge of making sure everyone on board was comfortable. Leo also heard this voyage would be his last, as the Cunard line was forcing him to retire at the age of 54, although he didn't want to.

With gray hair and a gray mustache, he stood proud and distinguished in his neatly trimmed white uniform. Mr. Jones took pride in presenting himself *perfectly* to the passengers.

"I just spoke to the bridge, and I have yesterday's mileage in," Mr. Jones announced.

The room leaned in, very curious, and listened attentively. Mrs. Beauclerk leaned back and motioned for Martha and Leo to come over. "Everyone's been placing bets on how far we go each day," she explained. "There's nothing these people won't place bets over!"

Mr. Jones knew he had the attention of the room, and his white mustache gleefully smiled at this fact. "Yesterday," he announced, "Lusitania sailed 509 nautical miles."

The room erupted into a chaos of both groans and cheers. But Leo was confused.

509? That wasn't right. That wasn't enough.

Leo did some quick calculating in his head. Lusitania could easily do twenty-eight or twenty-nine knots, or nautical miles in an hour. At twenty-nine knots, in twenty-four hours, Lusitania should have sailed over seven hundred nautical miles.

509? Something was wrong. That was too slow.

Leo did some more math in his head. To do 509 miles yesterday, Lusitania sailed at only twenty-one knots per hour.

That was too slow. Why only twenty-one, when she could do twenty-eight, or even twenty-nine?

Leo dashed out of the lounge. He had to find out why. He would return Mrs. Beauclerk's trunk to the cargo hold, and then head to the bridge to see if he could ask someone why they were going so slow.

Through the outside windows, Clyde worked on scrubbing the section of deck he had been assigned to clean that morning. The sight of Leo dashing out of the First Class lounge caught his eye. Leo wasn't supposed to be there! Why was Leo allowed so much freedom? What made him so special?

Why had no one fired Leo for leaving all the nets loose in the cargo hold?

Clyde dropped his broom. It was time to find out.

Chapter 11

The air in Lusitania's corridors grew thick and stuffy as Leo descended deeper down her decks. Lusitania was one of the first giant ships, five years older than *Titanic* and her identical sister *Olympic*. Leo huffed the muggy air, wishing the ship's designers had found a better way to get fresh air this deep into the ship.

He pushed Mrs. Beauclerk's trunk down the hallway to the forward cargo hold. The crew-only section of the ship was not as decorative as her quarters on B Deck, and a string of lightbulbs dimly illuminated the passage. His footsteps and the squeak of the cart echoed off the walls.

He pushed open the door to the forward cargo hold and stood, astonished.

The room, full of bags, boxes, and trunks, was a mess! Piles of cargo lay on the floor, toppled down and strewn all over the place!

Leo left this room in perfect condition not an hour ago. Everything was tied down under nets to keep it from...

Clyde.

Leo realized he didn't leave the room perfect. He left Clyde behind.

He barely knew Clyde and he didn't know what Clyde had against him… but this was Clyde's doing.

He pushed the trunk into the room, slammed the door shut, and turned back down the crew hallway. Clyde would pay for this.

Leo rolled up his sleeves as he marched down the hallway.

But then, he stopped.

He stood there, breathing heavily.

No.

Leo knew that *he* was the better sailor. He desperately wanted to work on Lusitania. Fighting would just get him dismissed.

From now on, Leo would make sure Clyde couldn't undo his good work. He would make sure his work was impeccable. Captain Turner would certainly notice. Then Leo would be an officer soon enough, and *he* could dismiss Clyde.

He took a few slow, deep breaths, and then turned back down the dark hallway to the cargo hold. It would take him a while, but he could put everything back in order, and secure the nets.

The trunks and boxes were heavy. The cranes on the top deck lowered them down when they were brought aboard the ship. It took all of Leo's strength as he grunted to get the boxes back into place. And he had to work quickly. If the ship hit another wave before he had everything secured under nets, it would all come tumbling down again.

Clyde sneakily entered and shut the door behind him. Carefully and quietly, he tip-toed around to where Leo stacked boxes, and crept up behind his back.

"Hey!" Clyde shouted! Then, before Leo realized what was happening, Clyde shoved him and he fell to the ground!

Leo turned around, laying on his back, confused. "*I'm* the top seaman here," Clyde shouted, towering over him. "What makes *you* so special?"

Leo jumped to his feet. He wanted to fight back! He was ready. He was strong. He knew how to fight.

But something inside told him not to.

"What makes you so special?" Clyde egged him on. But Leo said nothing, did nothing.

"I have to organize the hold," Leo said, ignoring him.

"Yeah, because *you* left the nets loose?" Clyde mocked.

Leo ignored him. He wouldn't take Clyde's bait, no matter how hard Clyde tried. He turned, picked up another crate, and started building his stack.

But Clyde wouldn't accept Leo not fighting. He was itching for a fight, determined to get Leo to throw the first punch. He took a step closer to Leo and shoved him.

"I'll have you dismissed," Clyde mocked. "I have that authority."

Leo knew he was lying. But why? Why was Clyde so mad at him?

Clyde shoved him again, and his back screamed in pain! He landed hard on the shelf behind him.

But, no. He wanted to work on Lusitania. He would *not* fight Clyde, even though every part of his body wanted to. His arms were ready, waiting for his brain to give the order.

Then, the door to the hold opened. Two sailors, able-bodied seamen like Leo and Clyde, walked in, not expecting to see two of their fellow sailors battling.

"Hey!" one of them shouted, seeing Clyde pushing Leo. "Hey! Stop!"

But Clyde didn't stop. He pushed some more. He pushed Leo so hard that he fell!

And then everything went black.

Chapter 12

May 4, 1915

"Masterson!"

Did yesterday even happen? His excursion into the First Class lounge? The fight with Clyde in the hold?

"Masterson!"

Isn't this how he was woken up yesterday? Did yesterday even happen?

Third Officer Bestic towered over Leo in bed. Leo blinked, and blinked again. His world was still blurry.

"There you go, chap, come to."

Leo didn't recognize that voice. Was it Irish? His vision cleared a bit, and he didn't recognize the room. Where was he?

"Hello, good morning, young lad, wake up now!"

Finally, Leo blinked and shook the blurriness loose. His vision became clear. He saw Third Officer Bestic standing with a tall man in a white suit.

"There you go," the man said. "That's a good lad. I'm Doctor McDermott."

"You took a hard hit to the head," Officer Bestic continued. "But the doctor here says you'll be alright."

Leo sat up in his bed. The white walls made him think he was in the doctor's office. "What happened?" Leo asked.

"It seems Clyde attacked you in the cargo hold," Bestic explained. "Two of your lads walked in and stopped him, but not before he got you on the floor."

"What'd you do to make that fool so mad at you?" Doctor McDermott asked.

Bestic smiled. "You're just a really good sailor, that's what. Some people just can't handle it."

The cargo hold.

Leo remembered! It was a mess! And it was his fault for not making sure everything was secure before he left!

He jumped out of his bed. "I'm sorry sir," he rambled, "I need to get back to the cargo hold. The crates aren't secure!"

Bestic and the doctor just stood back and chuckled. "Son, your mates have the cargo secured for you, not to worry," Bestic explained.

"And the Master at Arms has Clyde all locked away, so you don't need to worry about him either."

Leo raised an eyebrow in confusion. "You mean, they cleaned up the cargo hold for me?"

Bestic smiled. "They did. You're a good chap. They just wanted to help."

Leo smiled. Maybe he would be alright. Maybe he would get to stay on Lusitania after all! He was certainly glad he didn't punch Clyde himself.

"Oh," Bestic continued, "and Captain Turner would like to see you on the bridge when you're all feeling better."

Feeling better? Just the thought of Captain Turner wanting to see *him* made him feel fantastic!

"Yes, yes!" he shouted. "Let's go!"

***

The bridge. For an aspiring sailor like Leo, the bridge is where he wants to be. The bridge is where the captain and his officers control the ship.

The captain and his officers.

Only the officers. Not people like Leo.

But Officer Bestic led Leo down the boat deck towards the bow. Maybe someday Leo would stand on the bridge of his own ship. He could only imagine! He smiled as he walked past other seamen scrubbing coal soot off the boat deck. He may as well have been captain already!

Bestic opened a small gate that separated the officer's promenade deck from the passengers and led Leo through. Lusitania's bridge curved around the front of the ship, and two wings extended off the side. Leo remembered seeing the captain standing on the bridge wing when leaving New York, looking out over the side of the ship.

The curved bridge gracefully wrapped around the front of the boat deck. Large windows filled the front, giving the officers a commanding view of the ship's bow and the sea in front of them.

Below the windows, large, circular telegraph machines let the officers communicate with the engine room. The officers used levers on the telegraph dials to send the engine room the speed they wanted. For each of the four propellers, Leo could see the speed ordered by the bridge: *Ahead Full*.

If the engines are set to Ahead Full, Leo thought, *then they must not have all the boilers lit. We're certainly not making full speed.*

The back of the bridge held another room, the Wheelhouse. The bridge itself was open to the outside, but the wheelhouse is where the helmsman actually steered the ship, and it was enclosed and heated.

Leo looked around. He didn't see Captain Turner, but the other officers on duty stood, monitoring the compass and the sea in front of them. Three of Lusitania's nine officers rotated eight-hour shifts. While on duty, the officers were not allowed to sit.

"The captain's on his way up," Bestic told Leo. "You just wait here."

Leo smiled. He wasn't going anywhere.

Behind them, Leo saw a table full of maps that marked their progress, as well as the log they used to record anything notable. Leo studied the map of the Atlantic. With this being their third full day at sea, they were just about halfway to England.

But then, he remembered: they only sailed just over five hundred miles yesterday. At full speed, Lusitania could nearly do seven hundred! He wasn't sure if he was supposed to read the log book, but he inched closer anyway.

Sure enough, for May 2nd and 3rd, Lusitania sailed only just around five hundred miles.

Why so slow? Leo thought.

A shadow covered his view of the book. A strong voice bellowed from the shadow. "Seeing anything interesting, son?"

Leo turned around to see Captain Turner standing behind him. All of the sudden, Leo didn't know what to say! "Oh, um, well, um... hi, sir, Captain, sir," he stammered.

Captain Turner showed Leo a kind smile, and put his strong hand on Leo's shoulder. "I heard you got in a tussle with one of your crewmates," he said. "I'm glad you're doing alright."

Leo sheepishly looked at the floor. Truthfully, it was actually a little bit embarrassing. "Thank you, sir," he said.

"Did you and Mister Bisset get enough practice lowering the boats yesterday?" the captain asked.

Leo couldn't tell if the captain couldn't remember Bestic's name, or just simply didn't care to. "Yes," he replied, "yes we did."

"Well, good then. Feel free to stand watch here on the bridge here until your shift starts, Seaman Masterson." Then, he winked at Leo, and turned away.

"Um, sir!" Leo blurted, and then immediately regretted it as the other officers on the bridge turned to look at him as well. Captain Turner stopped in his spot and turned to face Leo, without saying anything.

To even ask the question took courage. Leo wanted to show his curiosity without seeming to question the captain's decisions. "Why are we only making twenty-one knots?" he asked, almost shaking in his boots. "Aren't we capable of making twenty-eight, even twenty-nine?"

The captain smiled again. Standing straight up with his arms crossed behind him, he purposefully stepped over to the logbook. The captain of a ship always took heavy, purposeful steps.

Studying the logbook and the maps, he asked Leo, without turning back toward him, "Familiar with navigation, are you?" After a moment, he extended his hand, and gestured for Leo to come join him.

"Son, there's a coal shortage because of the war," he explained. "The battleships need all the coal. We've been instructed not to light all our boilers in order to save coal. We'll use thousands of tons less on this voyage because of it."

Then, Captain Turner pointed up to the map, to a small point on the south tip of Ireland. "To get to Liverpool," he explained, using his finger to trace the path on the map, "We need to sail around Ireland, and I've been instructed to stay away from shore. We'll sail right by here, *Old Head of Kinsale*."

His finger traced their route, and stopped over Liverpool, their destination. The port wasn't right on the ocean, but just a short way inland. "And then we'll squeeze into Liverpool," he explained. "What do you know about tides, Masterson?"

"I know about high tide and low tide," Leo answered. "The water level goes up and down during the day. High tide is when the water is the highest."

Captain Turner nodded. "We can only enter Liverpool at high tide, or we'll run aground and the ship will hit the bottom of the bay. If we go any faster than we are now, we'll arrive too early and have to wait."

Then, he turned and looked Leo directly in the eye. "*That's* when the submarines could get us," Turner explained. "We monitor our speed every day to make sure we enter Liverpool right at high tide, so we don't need to stop."

He turned away from Leo and stared out the large front windows for a few moments. "I need to be on my rounds, Seaman Masterson. I'll leave you to your duties." And with that, the captain walked off the bridge, and strolled down the boat deck.

What an impossible problem, Leo thought. Lusitania's speed was her biggest advantage to keep safe from submarines. But, going *too fast* would get them to Liverpool too early, and she would have to come to a complete stop and wait to enter the harbor.

Maybe Leo *didn't* want to be a captain after all. Captain Turner's job now seemed quite impossible.

Chapter 13

May 5, 1915

Lightbulbs. Burned out lightbulbs everywhere. Leo quickly learned that Lusitania constantly burned through lightbulbs. Maybe it was because electricity was still new when the ship was built. Maybe it was because the constant vibration of the engines was too much for the delicate pieces inside the bulbs. But, nonetheless, the constant need to change lightbulbs kept Leo very busy.

Leo walked down the stairs to B Deck. At the bottom of the B Deck stairs, the Purser's Desk seemed almost like a bank. Two officers stood behind a windowed desk, and passengers stood in line to talk to them.

Leo walked past the deck, and the busy Purser waved at him. The burned out bulb Leo was there to replace was inside the purser's office, and the officer knew why he was there.

A first class man stood at the desk, arguing with the purser. Snooping was wrong, and he knew it, but he couldn't help but listen to the passenger's complaints as he replaced the lightbulb.

"What do you mean I can't send out a wireless?" the man asked, very angry.

"Cunard Line orders, sir. I'm very sorry," the purser explained. It didn't seem to calm the passenger much.

"How does Cunard expect me to be able to communicate with my business ashore if I can't send out wireless messages? That's why I sailed on Lusitania in the first place!"

The purser again politely nodded. "Cunard Line orders. I'm very sorry."

The man pounded his fist on the table. "Then, may I ask, what is the purpose of having a wireless aboard this ship, if you can't use it?" he asked, though he didn't seem much interested in the answer.

"Because," the purser explained, "we can receive messages, but if we send messages, German submarines can use our signal to determine our location." Then the purser, clearly tired of the man's arrogance, leaned in and asked, "We wouldn't want that now, would we?"

It's not usually Cunard Line policy to embarrass a first class passenger. But now, the man was quite embarrassed by his show, and at his insistence in putting the whole ship in danger for his own benefit.

"Yes, of course," the man now sheepishly answered. "My apologies."

Leo tried not to look like he was paying attention as the man turned and walked away. Now, the purser turned to other passengers. He was sure to repeat the same conversation with more passengers who wanted to send messages to their homes or businesses. Other passengers wanted their money or jewels stored in the purser's safe. But, the purser had a few people in line, and had to deal with them quickly and politely.

Now that Leo saw the type of light bulb he needed to replace, he left the office and walked down the main staircase down to the supply room on F Deck.

Walking down the hallway, he passed a bunk room like his own. But something caught his eye, and he stopped, and looked inside.

It was Clyde. He was handcuffed to the bed. Leo felt a small surge of energy jolt through his body. He didn't know what Clyde's problem with him was, but he couldn't resist the urge to stand in the doorway - out of Clyde's reach - and rub it in.

"Spending the rest of the voyage down here?" Leo bragged. "It's a shame. This is a beautiful ship."

Clyde didn't seem interested in talking to him. He rolled over in bed as much as he could, away from Leo. But Leo kept going. He couldn't help it. He realized he knew why Clyde hated him - Leo was the better sailor. Clyde was used to being the top man, and now Leo came aboard and was better.

That realization filled Leo with pride. He had to rub it in.

"You know, I got to work on the bridge today?" Leo gloated. "Have you ever worked on the bridge?" Then, he stepped in, just out of reach of Clyde's bunk. "I guess we both got what we deserve: me on the bridge and you in the brig."

He tapped Clyde's handcuffs, and then strolled out of the room. But, in the hallway, his energy dropped. He didn't feel good.

That was mean, Leo thought. He shouldn't have done that. He wasn't a mean person.

But he wouldn't go back in to apologize. He had work to do.

Chapter 14

May 6th, 1915

The only clothes Martha carried onto Lusitania were three sets of her black and white maid's uniform, and one pair of pajamas. And so, like always, she wore her black and whites as she and Mrs. Beauclerk walked down the enclosed promenade. The sun set behind the ship on the far side of the Atlantic. Lusitania's propellers left a long trail of churned up water as far as they could see. Martha dutifully followed Mrs. Beauclerk down the promenade deck back into the first class lounge.

But Mrs. Beauclerk stopped before she entered and clutched her stomach. She stooped over and braced herself against the door frame. Martha rushed to her side.

"Is everything alright, ma'am?" she asked.

But Mrs. Beauclerk said nothing, just squeezed her eyes. She stood, leaned over, in pain and breathing heavily. Martha looked around. Should she fetch the doctor? Was anyone else around who could help?

It was late and many passengers had already retired to their rooms, but Mrs. Beauclerk wanted to chat in the lounge with a few of her new friends.

Finally, whatever had gripped her released itself, and Mrs. Beauclerk relaxed to catch her breath. "I don't like what the spirits are telling me, Martha," she sounded worried. "I wish we had missed this ship."

Then, she pushed open the swinging door, and entered the lounge. The magnificent skylight above scattered the last few rays of sunshine, as the light bulbs took over lighting up the room in their orange glow.

A few men read, a few women sat on couches and gossipped. Mrs. Beauclerk headed over to the fireplace and joined a group led by

Alfred Vanderbilt, still dressed in his tuxedo from dinner.

"Good of you to join us, Lizzie," he excitedly greeted her.

She didn't answer, but just sat down.

A piano player played some lively music in the background. On the other end of the room, some passengers even seemed to be having a talent show, and the crowd gathered around a man doing some sort of card trick. They laughed when he made a mistake!

Any start to a conversation was interrupted by Captain Turner coming through the doorway. It was unlike him to join the passengers in the lounge. The hushed conversation and quiet card games all stopped the moment the captain entered the room. Captain Turner could command the room's attention without asking for it.

It was customary for the captain to remove his hat when he entered a room, and he did so this evening. But, his blue eyes seemed worried. The room absorbed his tense energy.

"Good evening, ladies and gentlemen," he announced. He paused, and everyone waited.

"Tomorrow morning," he continued, "we will be entering waters off the coast of Ireland declared a war zone by Germany."

Martha watched the room as all the passengers turned toward each other, giving each other knowing glances. Truth is, they expected this. Submarines were all anyone could talk about! But they knew Lusitania could outrun any torpedo.

Or at least, they thought so.

"But not to worry," the captain comforted them. "By tomorrow, we will be securely in the care of the British Royal Navy. We'll bring you into Liverpool on time and safely."

Then, Captain Turner put his hat back on, and turned toward the door. "Enjoy your evening," he said to the room one last time, before heading back to the bridge.

It took a few moments for the room to return to normal. But return to normal it did. The conversation and card games resumed, the music played, and the talent show continued on the other side. It returned to normal for everyone but Mrs. Beauclerk, who excused herself and moved to sit on a lone couch by herself.

Martha, wanting to help, leaned in and whispered, "Shall we return to our room, ma'am?"

Mrs. Beauclerk simply closed her eyes and shook her head. "No, Martha. "We'll sleep in here tonight. I don't want to be trapped below decks when the torpedo hits."

So sure was Mrs. Beauclerk that a torpedo would indeed hit Lusitania, it was almost as if her mysterious spirits had shown her a photograph. Martha wondered exactly what this photograph looked like.

***

Captain Turner returned to the bridge, where Leo worked on painting a railing. Salt from the sea was the constant enemy of ships (besides submarines). There was always painting to do, to keep the sea from rusting the steel ship away.

"Seaman Masterson," Captain Turner called him over. Leo put down his brush and joined the captain. Together, they looked down the Boat Deck, toward the stern, toward the setting sun and the growing blackness of being alone in the middle of the ocean.

For a few moments, Captain Turner said nothing. They just listened to the sound of the bow slicing through the water, and the steam escaping the black funnels. After a few tense breaths, Captain Turner broke his silence. He didn't sound worried, but his voice showed he understood the seriousness of their situation. "You and Bestic gather up all the men you can," he instructed. "Very quietly, without disturbing the passengers, swing out all of the lifeboats and prepare them for launching."

Leo looked up at the captain, who just stared at the quickly shrinking glow of the sun on the horizon. With the sun's light no longer strong enough to illuminate the ship, Captain Turner looked worried under the glow of the orange electric lamps.

But he didn't say anything. He just turned, and walked toward the bridge.

Leo was proud to be able to execute the captain's orders. He went into the officer's quarters and awakened Officer Bestic. Together, they found all the free men they could find, from seamen, to stokers, and even cooks. Boat by boat, they worked their way down the boat deck.

For all twenty-two lifeboats, they removed the canvas covers, set the oars inside, and cranked the davits out so the boats hung over the side of the ship.

They worked swiftly and quietly. By midnight, should the worst happen, the boats could be lowered at a moment's notice.

Leo prayed the worst would not happen. He couldn't wait for morning, when he would awaken to find Lusitania escorted by a Royal Navy destroyer, working to keep them safe.

Chapter 15

May 7, 1915.

Blackness surrounded Lusitania as Leo went to bed. Captain Turner ordered all the windows closed, shades pulled, and outside lights turned off. The black ship was soon lost in the black sea under the black of night.

As morning arose, white replaced the blackness.

Pure white.

Fog.

Heavy, dense fog. The ship sailed through a cloud so thick the helmsman couldn't see the bow from the bridge.

Leo awoke. He didn't waste any time, and immediately went to the Seaman's Mess. He ate quickly, scarfing down some scrambled eggs, bacon, and toast. Then he rushed up to the boat deck.

A few passengers strolled the deck. They saw all the boats swung out for launching. "Not to worry, dear," Leo heard a man comforting his wife. "I'm sure it's all well and good."

But further down the deck, he spied another group of passengers wearing their life jackets. A few seemed confused by how to put on the puffy white vests. They all seemed like they were practicing, so that if something bad happened, they would know what to do.

Out of the corner of his eye, something unusual caught his attention. He looked down in one of the lifeboats swinging over the side of the ship. It seemed a man had chosen to sleep the rest of the night inside the lifeboat, while wearing his life jacket over his clothes.

"Leo!" he heard his voice from a distance. He turned around. Martha walked toward him, still in her black and white maid's uniform. "Leo!" she called again.

He stopped and waited. She seemed out of breath, and worried. "I just came from the lounge," she said. "Mrs. Beauclerk slept there all night. Submarines are all anyone's talking about! Do you think we'll be alright?"

Honestly, Leo didn't know. They weren't making full speed, certainly not in this fog. But he knew this passage past Ireland was the only way into Liverpool, and submarines were definitely on the hunt. All he could do was shrug his shoulders.

Suddenly, a loud boom jolted them! They jumped. The ship's horns blasted!

"What was that?" Martha shrieked.

"Fog horns," Leo explained. "They can't see, so they're listening for echoes and letting other ships know we're here."

Martha's eyes grew wide. "Other ships? Like submarines?"

Again, Leo shrugged.

"What do we do if we're hit?" Martha asked. Her voice begged Leo to say something that made her feel better.

"Get to a lifeboat," he answered.

Martha pointed to the one they were standing next to on the starboard side. "I'll bring Mrs. Beauclerk to this one," she said.

Leo nodded. "That's number five."

"Why is that five?" Martha asked, confused.

"The ones on the starboard side are the odd numbers," Leo explained, pointing to them in order. "One, three, five."

Officer Bestic interrupted them. "Masterson!" he called, "All the seamen are being called to the bridge."

Martha hugged Leo. A giant, hard, worried hug. "Be safe, Leo," she begged.

"Boat number five," he reminded her, before turning to walk to the bridge with Bestic.

Martha shuddered as the fog horn rang out again.

***

On the bridge, Captain Turner stood in the doorway of the wheelhouse. "Stay on this course, Johnston," he instructed the quartermaster at the helm. In the fog, all they could do to navigate was guess. The team of officers on the bridge kept track of their speed and direction, and traced the path they *thought* they were taking on the maps. But until the fog cleared, they would not know for sure where they were.

Then, the captain came out to address the small team of blue-uniformed seamen. "Gentlemen," he said, "You see the fog. We need to post extra lookouts."

One by one, he pointed to them. Two, he sent to the very front of the bow. Two more, further back on the bow deck along the railings. He pointed to Leo. "Masterson," he ordered, "Watch off the starboard bridge wing."

Leo nodded. His station was close. He turned around, and took watch as far as he could press himself onto the edge of the bridge wing. He was hanging over the side of the ship. But, when he looked down, the fog was so thick he couldn't even see the water.

At the very least, he thought, *we're more in danger of a blind submarine running into us than torpedoing us.*

Chapter 16

Captain Walter Schweiger looked through the periscope of his submarine, the U-20. The fog had broken. He kept his submarine just under the water, and his small periscope popped up just above the surface. He could see land, but he couldn't see any ships.

When U-20 began their journey from Germany a few weeks ago, they were loaded with ten torpedoes. Now, with only two left, it was almost time to go home. He liked to save two torpedoes for the journey home. But, now that the fog cleared, he wanted to stay off the coast of Ireland for just a few more hours, just to see what might come by.

He spun his periscope around, looking in all directions across the water and on the bright Irish coast, while his tired crew waited below. When a submarine stays under water, the air quickly becomes humid, hot, and stinky.

They measured their success in tonnage sunk. The more ships they sank, the more successful their voyage was. This voyage of the U-20 was a dismal failure. Eight torpedoes launched, and only two tiny freighters to show for it. The tired crew was ready to go home.

Captain Schweiger again spun his periscope. In the distance, coming over the horizon, he spotted a large, black smoke trail.

***

The passengers and crew of Lusitania were relieved when the fog cleared. The sight of the Irish coast off their port side comforted them. And, on the bridge, Captain Turner and Officer Bestic smiled when they spotted a familiar landmark in their binoculars.

"There!" Turner announced. "Kinsale Head." Just over the horizon, a small bit of land jutted out from the Irish coast. The towers from an old castle stood on the tip of the island. "Fix our exact position," Turner instructed Bestic. "I need to use the lavatory in my cabin for a few minutes."

Leo still remained on watch on the starboard bridge wing, but he heard the captain's footsteps as he left the bridge. "Set course to eighty-seven degrees East. Note the time in the log, Kinsale Head at 1:40," the captain ordered as he walked away.

Immediately, as the helmsman turned to starboard, Leo felt the ship make the turn to the right.

***

Captain Schweiger kept his periscope fixed on the large black smoke trail. It came closer to the U-20, and now he could make out four black funnels!

He blinked. *Could it be?* he thought. Every U-Boat captain studied pictures of British ships, from war ships to passenger liners. He could recognize any British ship simply from its small, black silhouette. There was no doubt in his mind the ship that now sailed straight for him.

"Prepare a forward torpedo," he ordered in German. His crew immediately leapt into action. No one but Captain Schweiger could see anything outside their submarine. They did as they were instructed. Their captain seemed excited.

In his head, Captain Schweiger tried to calculate the speed and direction of the oncoming ship, but the ship changed direction and sailed away.

He kept watching.

***

Now that Officer Bestic had determined Lusitania's exact position, Quartermaster Johnston at the helm began the new maneuver Cunard instructed them to perform when they neared England: The *Zig Zag*. He would steer left for a few minutes, and then steer right for a few minutes. The Zig Zag would keep submarines from being able to determine their exact speed and direction.

As the Lusitania zig zagged through the water, Leo looked off in the distance and noticed something missing. They were supposed to be protected by destroyers from the Royal Navy.

But no such ship followed them. Lusitania was alone.

***

Captain Schweiger called another crew member up to the periscope. He recognized the ship in his sights, but he wanted to be sure.

The dirty and sweaty crewman looked through the periscope for only a few moments, then looked back to the captain.

"Is it?" the captain asked.

The crewman only nodded his head, but the captain already knew. He looked back through the periscope, and he saw the Lusitania make a sudden right turn.

This was it. It was almost like the ship turned on purpose to give the U-20 a perfect shot. "Bear right, ten degrees," he called to his pilot. He needed not to aim for where Lusitania was now, but to where it would be forty seconds after he fired the torpedo. He calculated the math in his head.

"Torpedo armed and ready, sir!" His torpedo crew called out from below.

One more time, Captain Schweiger checked his math. He guessed his distance from the ship, and knew the speed his torpedoes traveled. Once the torpedo burst free from its tube, it would be forty seconds before he knew it hit. If he was right.

But, he knew he was right. With Lusitania's black smoke cloud growing in his periscope about half a mile away, Captain Schweiger called out his order:

"Fire."

Chapter 17

Lusitania's passengers tried not to act worried. They day had grown beautiful, and many of them strolled about the decks for their after lunch walks. Seagulls from the Irish coast curiously flew around the ship's masts.

Leo rubbed his heavy eyes, weary from standing on the bridge for three hours. At first, he watched through the fog for other ships. Now, he looked over the water for any sign of a submarine.

It started with a small glimmer. In the calm water, about half a mile away, a splash. Leo didn't hear anything, but he saw what he thought was a fish jumping out of the water.

He watched the spot.

It wasn't a fish.

A thin, straight trail of bubbles grew from the splash. He squinted, and tried to see it better.

***

Mrs. Beauclerk reserved her deck chair on the first day of the voyage. She laid in her chair on the starboard promenade deck, her arm over her eyes, breathing heavily. Martha, worried, stood behind her.

"The spirits, Martha," Mrs. Beauclerk whimpered. "Make them stop!"

Martha didn't know what to do. Mrs. Beauclerk seemed to be drowning in terror, beyond any help!

Nearby, a group of nicely-dressed women, in gowns and flashy hats, stood along the railing. Suddenly, they murmured. Their murmurs grew louder and they pointed out over the water.

Then Martha heard one woman's voice very clearly. It was funny how first-class women never sounded panicked, but more curious than alarmed. The woman simply tilted her head and softly asked, "Why, that's a torpedo, isn't it?"

***

Leo couldn't believe his eyes. What should he do? He wasn't even sure what it was. He didn't want to make a mistake! But it only took a few seconds for the narrow trail of bubbles to grow longer and longer.

He shouted. He shouted with the loudest, most urgent, most panic he had ever shouted in his life. "TORPEDO COMING ON THE STARBOARD SIDE!"

And then nothing happened. The trail in the water raced closer, but the ship did nothing. The officers on the bridge curiously turned toward Leo. Did they not hear him?

Then, another shout from the Crow's Nest above the ship. "Torpedo! Starboard side, sir!"

But there was nothing that could be done. Before anyone else could react, before Quartermaster Johnston could turn the helm, and before the engines could be ordered into reverse, it happened.

Leo watched in horror as the bubble trail raced toward the ship.

It hit the starboard side and exploded with such force the whole ship rocked back and forth, as if God himself pushed Lusitania around like a toy! A massive spout of water and fire shot upwards into the lifeboats. Lifeboat number five burst into splinters as the water rammed through it. Water and splinters rained down on the deck on top of the passengers gathered by the railing.

Then, quickly, another explosion. This one was different. It came from inside. Cold sea water rushing in and hitting the red-hot boilers instantly erupted into steam and destroyed the forward boiler room. Leo looked up and saw black soot and steam shooting out of the first funnel!

The explosion knocked Leo off his feet. He lay on the ground on the bridge wing.

Quickly, he picked himself up and ran toward the bridge. But, he noticed, something was off: the bridge was *uphill*.

He made it to the bridge at the same time as Captain Turner. "Was it a torpedo?" the captain shouted.

"It was, yes sir," Quartermaster Johnston shouted from the helm. "She's listing ten degrees!"

That's why Leo felt like he was running uphill. The ship was leaning ten degrees already! The damage from the torpedo had to be massive.

"Bear north and try to run aground on Kinsale Head!" Captain Turner commanded.

Smart move, Leo thought. The captain was trying to run the ship aground before it sank. But, it wouldn't work.

"Helm is not responding, sir!" Johnston shouted. His attempts to turn the ship's wheel weren't turning the ship. The torpedo had done too much damage. "List is at fifteen degrees!"

"Keep trying," Turner answered, but he knew it was for naught.

It was time to abandon ship.

But Lusitania still moved too fast! Lowering the lifeboats into the water while the ship was still in motion was dangerous. They needed to bring the ship to a stop.

"All engines full reverse," the captain ordered. Officers immediately raced to the telegraph machines. Bells in the telegraphs chimed as officers pushed the signal levers into the *Full Reverse* positions. They waited for the engine room to respond that the engines had been reversed.

The signal never came.

All Lusitania could do was drift to a stop. The crew could no longer control her. Only nature now held Lusitania's fate.

The officers on the bridge turned to Captain Turner. There was only one order left to give:

"Abandon ship."

Chapter 18

The passengers knew what to do. Whether or not they chose to admit it, they had been waiting for this moment. Their imaginations already planned how they would react.

Every staircase filled with passengers racing up the stairs to the boat deck. Their progress was slow and clumsy. The ship listed heavily, and the explosion knocked out all the electricity. Passengers tripped over each other as they ran up uneven stairs in complete darkness.

One deck below the boat deck, Mrs. Beauclerk sat paralyzed in her deck chair. Her eyes froze with fear as men and women and children ran past her.

"Mrs. Beauclerk!" Martha begged. "Lizzie, please, we have to go!" She shoved a life jacket onto Mrs. Beauclerk's lap.

But her lady was too scared, too afraid to move. It was almost as if the explosion had turned her into stone.

"Please, Lizzie!" Martha screamed. "We have to go up to boat number five!"

She grabbed Mrs. Beauclerk's arm, but couldn't move her. She pulled and pulled, but the terrified Mrs. Beauclerk wouldn't budge.

More passengers ran by, screaming, pouring out of every doorway and fighting to get to the stairs. With every passing moment, the bow of the ship sank further into the water. Lusitania didn't have long to live. Maybe just minutes, certainly not hours.

Martha's heart sank. She let go of Mrs. Beaucklerk's arm, and then took her own life jacket and slipped it over her head. She made for her what was an impossible, heartbreaking decision.

"I'll be on boat number five," she said to Mrs. Beauclerk, who still didn't acknowledge her. Martha pleaded one final time, "Get to a boat, Lizzie!" Then, Martha turned and joined the running, screaming crowd, racing to the stairway.

A sea of people streamed up the stairways. Suddenly, the ship lurched! The sudden movement threw people to their feet. The decks erupted in more screams.

"I always thought the sinking of a ship was an orderly thing," the lady in front of Martha quipped.

"So did I," Martha replied, "but I've learned a devil of a lot in the last five minutes."

Nearly up the stairs, Martha took one last look at the promenade deck behind her, and Mrs. Beauclerk, still sitting on her deck chair.

Up a few more stairs, she reached the crowded boat deck, and gasped!

Lifeboat number five was gone.

And she couldn't see Leo anywhere.

Chapter 19

Abandon ship.

Since boarding Lusitania, Leo acted like he knew everything. But he didn't know this. He didn't know what to do.

Things were happening too fast, orders being shouted about from officers without anyone to respond to them!

Leo felt a strong hand grab his arm. Officer Bestic grabbed him and yanked him off the bridge! "Come on," Bestic barked, rapidly. "Port side, with me. Grab as many men as you can."

Leo and Bestic raced through the bridge to the port side of the ship. The crowd of passengers didn't know what to do! Some of them were already jumping into lifeboats. Bestic threw him in front of boat number two.

"You're in charge of number two!" Bestic shouted.

"Me?"

"We need to get them down quickly! Go!"

Leo rushed to his place, trying to find men - any men at all - who could help him lower his boat. But then, he noticed a problem: the ship was listing too far to starboard. The boats on the port side rested against the side of the ship! If they tried to lower them, the rivets that stuck out from the side of Lusitania's hull would rip them to shred!

It was impossible to lower any boats from the port side!

"Sir!" Leo shouted over the screaming crowd. "We can't lower these! It's listing too much!"

Captain Turner's second-in-command, Staff Captain Anderson, ran over to supervise the port side boats. He saw Bestic and Leo, and right away saw the problem.

"Bestic, go to the bridge and tell them to trim her with the port ballast tanks!" Anderson shouted. If his plan worked, they would flood the port side on purpose in order to level out the ship. Bestic nodded, and ran away to the bridge.

Then, screams from behind him startled Leo. The screaming passengers looked out not over the water, but inward at the ship. Men climbed out of the large, brown vents on the boat deck that fed fresh air to the boiler rooms. The men were dirty, wet, and covered with coal soot. They looked like demons rising up from the dead.

But one, he recognized. George!

"George!" Leo shouted. "George!"

His friend heard him, and ran over. "Leo! You're alive!"

"What's it like down there?"

George shook his head. He knew Lusitania was doomed. "Black. Boiler room's already flooded. Starboard coal bunker flooded instantly. She's going down fast!"

Then, George saw boat two resting against Lusitania's deck. "You can't lower it like that!" he exclaimed. "It'll scrape the rivets on the hull and rip the boat to shreds!"

"They're going to flood the port ballast tanks," Leo hollered.

George again shook his head. "It won't work," he shuddered. "Everyone who would do that is already up here. And I think there's a lot of good men still trapped down there."

Then Leo remembered: Clyde. Clyde was under arrest, handcuffed to a bunk below decks.

In the chaos, had anyone remembered to free him?

Chapter 20

Martha frantically ran about the boat deck. "Leo!" She called out. "Leo!" The screams of people scrambling to the boats drowned out her own. Officers bellowed orders, but no one heard them over the roar of the crowd.

She couldn't find Leo. She told him she would be in boat number five, but it wasn't there! She looked across the water. It hadn't been launched yet. It had just disappeared!

Last she knew, Leo was on the bridge. She ran toward the front of the ship, trying to keep her balance despite the ship's hard lean. "Leo!" She called out again, but her brother was nowhere to be seen.

She turned around, and she couldn't run to the other side. There were too many people! She had to push and shove. "Leo!" She kept calling out.

Crowds grew around boats number seven and nine. By boat eleven, in the middle of the ship, the crowd was too thick, and she couldn't get through.

She pushed her way to the front of the deck and stared at the empty boat number eleven! Despite the crowd, despite the danger, despite the rapidly sinking ship, no one was in it! She quickly figured out why: the ship was leaning so far over that the boat hung six feet away from the boat deck. Anyone wanting to get in the boat would have to jump over open water!

No railing protected the passengers crowding the edge of the deck from the open sea below. The water rushed by as the Lusitania coasted to a long stop. The increasing tilt of the deck threatened to dump everyone off anyway, so Martha decided to go for it!

"Stand back!" she shouted. The crowd stepped back as much as they could, shoving the people furthest back into the walls. Martha's thick white life jacket pushed down the fluff from her maid's outfit. With a deep breath, she leaned down and put her right foot forward.

She burst into motion!

One step.

Two steps.

Three steps.

Leap!

Martha flew across the open water, her ruffles fluttering in the air behind her. With a *thud*, she landed in the center of the wooden boat between two rows of benches. The cork in her life jacket cushioned her landing.

I made it, she thought, as breathed a sigh of relief. Surely Leo saw her, and was coming to boat eleven as well?

More passengers, inspired by Martha's bravery, took running jumps themselves. She reached out to grab their hands and help them in, should they miss and wind up clinging to the side of the boat.

More women and men took running jumps. Ten, fifteen, twenty. Though the boat could hold seventy, there wasn't room for more than twenty to land safely after jumping for their lives from Lusitania's doomed deck.

"STOP!" called out the officer in charge of the boat. Two crew members, filthy enough that Martha assumed they worked in the boiler rooms, jumped on the ropes holding the boat to the davits and climbed down into the boat.

"Lower it!" the officer called out. He shouted to the stokers now positioned at the front and back, "Take on more when you're in the water!"

The stokers nodded and, with a startling jolt, the boat came loose. Two crewmen on the deck feverishly worked the ropes, and the boat quickly jerked and shuddered its way down the remaining twenty feet to the water.

Twenty feet was far too little.

Everyone in the boat knew: Lusitania had only minutes to live. Boat eleven was the first one to go.

It might even be the last.

Chapter 21

By now, the stairwell on C Deck was clear. All the people had made their way up to the boat deck.

Almost everyone.

Leo was certain, so certain he felt a deep pull in his soul, that Clyde had been forgotten. Whatever he had done to Leo, however mean he had been, Leo knew Clyde didn't deserve to die.

But finding him would be another task. Deep within Lusitania, electric lights lit up the hallways. But the power was out. Lusitania's maze of hallways were completely black. Leo stepped on the landing to D Deck like a blind man. Only the muffled sound of screams above and the groans of Lusitania's straining steel reached his senses.

Noise, and fear. But nothing to see.

Think before you act, he remembered Martha warning him on the very first day of the voyage. *Think before you act*. Rushing down to rescue Clyde was impulsive. He hadn't thought.

But he would now.

On the B Deck landing, Leo caught a glimpse of a long, coiled-up fire hose. He took it.

On C Deck, another one. He took that one, too.

Past the D Deck landing on the main staircase was utter darkness. He had to get to F deck to rescue Clyde, and then forward, into the flooding.

If he could make his way back to the main staircase, even in darkness, he could *feel* his way back up. But, he would need a way to get back to the staircase.

In the blackness, he gripped the hoses with one hand and the railings with another. Usually, even his blind body could walk down stairs. But that's when the stairs are level. These stairs are on a sinking ship, leaning backward and sideways. He had to move slower than he wanted.

Too slow. Every moment longer it took him, Lusitania sank further into the sea.

Finally, no more stairs. F Deck. He tied the end of the fire hose to the railing and walked toward what he knew was forward. He knew it was forward because it was downhill.

It was still dry, and that's all Leo needed to know. He uncoiled the fire hose as he walked. "Clyde!" he screamed. "Clyde! Are you there!"

Down the tilted hallway, Leo walked with his left foot on the carpet and his right foot on the wall.

"Clyde! Clyde! Are you there!"

He walked carefully and listened. He heard nothing but surging water.

"Clyde! Scream for me!"

Then, he heard it. A muffled voice in the distance.

"Leo! Leo! I'm in here!"

Leo ran toward the voice, then jerked to a sudden stop. He had reached the end of his first fire hose. Quickly, he tied the ends of the two hoses together, and then ran toward the voice.

"Keep yelling, Clyde!" he shouted.

"I'm in here! Leo!"

Leo ran.

Suddenly, water. It felt like a puddle. The next step was ankle deep. The next step, up to his knee. Then, he was swimming.

"Leo! Leo! I'm in here!"

He reached Clyde's door. Thankfully, it was unlocked. He burst into the room, where Clyde had just a little bit of light from the porthole in his room.

Leo instantly saw a problem: the porthole was under water. And Leo didn't walk into the room; he swam in.

Clyde saw Leo's fire hose. "I think you've come to rescue me from the wrong emergency, mate," he quipped. "Gonna need a bucket!"

"It's to help us make our way back out!" Leo growled.

Clyde held up his wrist, still handcuffed to his bed. "You best save yourself," he trembled. "Unless you got a key?"

Chapter 22

There's no way they can fill this boat, George thought. The boat rested against Lusitania's hull, but they were going to try to lower it anyway.

Twenty or so women nervously sat on the benches of boat number two. Strangers clutched strangers for comfort, screaming for the crewmen to start lowering.

George and four other of the stokers who climbed through the air vent with him a few moments ago stood inside the boat with the oars in their hands. As the crew on the deck worked the ropes, they would push as hard as they could against Lusitania's side. They hoped they could push the boat far enough away from the rivets that it would reach the water unharmed.

"Lower away!" Officer Bestic cried from the deck above. Two seamen in blue uniforms that somehow still looked perfect worked the ropes through their hands, and the boat jerked into motion.

George strained against his oar and the crew pushed as hard as they could. It was working, but they had to work fast. Lusitania twisted and turned as she sank. With unsteady footing, the sailors lowered faster.

Suddenly, Lusitania lurched! Her forward motion came to an abrupt stop. People on the deck screamed in unison, the most chilling cry George had ever heard. His boat swung back and forth in the davits like a playground swing, and the terrified women joined the chorus of screams! George lost his footing, and the boat slammed against the side of the ship.

Lusitania's sudden stop was enough to make hundreds of people on the boat deck lose their balance all at once, and many fell down, including the crewman working the forward rope on boat two!

He fell, tumbled forward, and lost grip of his rope. The rope came loose and flew through the davit. The forward end of boat two fell forward, swung freely, and dumped all her escaping passengers into the sea below.

Chapter 23

"What was that?" Clyde shouted.

The ship's hull groaned and screamed as she came to a sudden, hard stop. Water in the room sloshed against the wall, pushing Leo with it. Leo cocked his head for a moment, distracted.

"Bulkhead collapsed?" Leo thought aloud, breathing heavily. "Maybe. I dunno."

"Great!" Clyde said, and pointed out the door as more water started rushing in. "And I think your way out just collapsed."

Leo looked around the room. He had come too far to *not* save Clyde... or himself. He had to free him, somehow.

Then, in the corner of the room, he saw his tool: a metal chair, just below the surface of the quickly rising water. He pushed off the wall behind him and swam to it.

With the chair in one hand, he dragged it back over to Clyde's bed and jammed the leg through the handcuff ring that held him to the bed frame.

"Stand back!" he ordered, and then twisted. He leaned down on the chair and used all his weight to twist. He twisted more and more, harder and harder, until the handcuff ring popped free!

"My god, mate, I love you!" Clyde hugged him. "I'm sorry for..."

"Save it for when we survive," Leo cut him off. Their way out was gone. He looked at the porthole, and shuddered.

"I can get us outta here," Leo said, "but you're not gonna like it."

Chapter 24

Captain Turner stood on the starboard bridge wing. *The captain always goes down with the ship*, the saying goes. But Captain Turner knew the moral of the tale: the captain should not try to save himself until he knew everyone on board was safe.

The torpedo hit Lusitania at 1:50. His pocket watch now read 2:00. In less than ten minutes, Lusitania's bow had already disappeared under the water. He would *never* know if everyone was safe. He doubted any of Lusitania would be left by 2:10.

As he stood on the bridge wing, he also knew a horrible truth: no one would be coming to help. Last September, the HMS Aboukir of the British Navy was sunk by a submarine. The HMS Cressy and the HMS Hogue, sailing nearby, rushed to help.

Unfortunately, the U-9 that sank the Aboukir waited for her rescuers to arrive, and then sank the Cressy and Hogue as well. In one day, one ghostly submarine sank three of Britain's finest warships.

Captain Turner knew the British Royal Navy's new orders: no ocean-going vessels could come to the rescue of a submarine attack. All he could do now was stand on his bridge and watch the lifeboats struggle to get away in time.

Captain Turner had never been a war captain. He had never sailed on a warship. But he knew, until this war, warships always saw their enemy coming.

Before steam, it was sails. You could see the enemy's sails for miles, and be ready when they caught you. To fight you, they would have to get close enough to see your face.

But that was before.

Lusitania was not a warship, and Turner was not a war captain. And now, his ship was the victim of war, sunk by an enemy he didn't see coming. He couldn't see their faces. He never even saw their ship!

The rules of war didn't just change; they vanished.

Like the ship that sunk him.

He remained standing on the bridge wing as the deck sank from under him, and the wash from the water carried him away into the open sea.

He wondered if his enemy could see his face.

***

Inside U-20, Captain Schweiger pulled his eyes away from his periscope. It was eerie, being able to spy on the doomed ship and her desperate passengers. It was wrong, and in a way, unhuman. Here, in the safety of the U-20, he was completely removed from the shouts and screams of Lusitania's passengers and crew. He heard only the sounds of his own ship.

He frowned, lowered his periscope, and ordered the U-20 to sail away. It was time to go home.

Chapter 25

Lowering boats on the port side was hopeless, Bestic realized. He looked forward and saw the bow and bridge already under water. His only way to the starboard side was through the abandoned First Class lounge.

He ran through, dodging the chairs and tables sliding forward, downhill to the front of the room. He jumped with each crack of the crashing furniture, but made it safely across. He threw open the door to the boat deck and ran into the crowd scurrying up the deck, fighting for refuge on Lusitania's stern.

Looking forward, not just the bow and the bridge, but half the first funnel and the base of the second were also under water. Lusitania's stern pointed high into the air!

Crews fought and struggled to lower boats fifteen and twenty one. Fifteen was in the middle of the ship, and already close to the water. In fact, they barely needed to lower - they just needed to cut it loose! Twenty one had a ways to go, and the crew struggled to keep their footing as the boat swung dozens of feet below the davits.

Bestic looked out over the water and, of Lusitania's twenty two lifeboats, saw only four -

FOUR! - boats full of people rowing in the water. He gasped! Lusitania had enough boats for everyone, but half were on the port side and unusable. The rest fell, collapsed, or overturned. Four in the water, two being lowered. A thousand people swimming. What to do?

Two seamen tried to hook up the collapsible previously stowed under boat eleven. Bestic ran over to them. They would never get it ready in time!

"Stop!" he called out. "Stop! Don't! Just unhook it and let it float."

He grabbed all the men he could and shoved them toward the four remaining collapsible boats still above water on the starboard side. "Unhook them and let them float away!" He shouted his orders above the cry of the crowd. "People in the water can swim to them and climb aboard!"

He ran away and left the men to carry out his orders. He ran as fast as he could, nearly stumbling and trying his best to stay upright and get back through the lounge to the port side. The port side still had plenty of boats and collapsibles that could be cut loose! Would he find enough crew to help him?

Chapter 26

Cold water quickly filled the bunk room. "Close the door!" Leo ordered Clyde, who rushed to swim over and forced the door shut. The room glowed in a soft green light from the porthole, now completely underwater.

Leo looked directly at Clyde, his eyes wide with experience and the terror of knowing what was about to come. "You won't like this," he warned, "but trust me, it'll work."

"I trust you," Clyde answered.

Leo pointed to the window. "I'm gonna open the porthole..."

"What!" Clyde blurted. "That's looney!"

Leo shook Clyde's shoulders. "It's the only way out!" he nearly shouted!

Clyde nodded, and Leo continued. "I'm going to open the porthole. Save your breath and don't fight it. After the room is *completely full*, we'll be able to swim out."

Both sailors now swam, only a few feet of air remained between their head and the ceiling. Clyde examined the window. "Are you sure?" he asked.

"I've done it before," Leo insisted. "Hold yourself against the outside wall. Don't fight it, just stay calm until the room is full."

They both swam to the outside wall, and clung to the ceiling rafters right above where they floated.

"Ready?" Leo asked, sure of his plan but still needing to hope it would work.

Clyde nodded, and gripped the rafters just a little harder. Leo took a few deep breaths and, with one hand still holding on to the rafters, unhooked the lock holding the pothole closed.

The porthole swung open with so much force it ripped the window right off its hinge! Water rushed into the room with so much pressure that the bunks in the way ripped out their floor screws and flew across the room.

Clyde and Leo clung to the rafters and took deep breaths as the water quickly rose. It took only moments for their air pocket to shrink from three feet, to two feet, to mere inches. They took their last breaths - deep breaths - and held them.

Then, the water changed. Leo remembered the familiar feeling from five years ago. The water suddenly became still. He reached out and grabbed Clyde's arm, his body looked blurry through the water. He yanked Clyde as hard as he could and forced him through the open window.

He put his hands on the sides of the round porthole and pushed his own body through. Together, Clyde and Leo swam upwards, toward the sun, and kicked as hard as they could.

F Deck, through which they emerged, was deep under water. They were deeper under the water than either of them had ever been. Leo's ears ached with the pressure! They kept swimming, but they had a long way to go.

It was far. Too far. The sunlight barely grew in the foggy water above them. Leo's lungs burned and every muscle in his body screamed for him to just take a breath! One breath!

But, he knew, he couldn't. He just held his breath, fighting his entire body, fighting to reach the surface.

Blackness grew around the edges of his vision. The fuzzy blackness crept inwards. He swam now in a race between the blackness around the outside of his vision and the white in the center. His arms struggled, and his kick languished. The blackness grew.

Then the blackness suddenly became all white! Pure white. The most brilliant white Leo had ever experienced! His lungs couldn't hold it anymore. He released the air inside and took a massive breath.

And he didn't die. He didn't inhale water. It was air. Air! He made it! He was on the surface! He was breathing air! He was alive!

He blinked and tried to clear the sea water out of his eyes. As his vision cleared, so did his hearing. He wasn't out of danger yet. Lusitania's stern still hung high above the water, but was quickly settling in. The screams of people still clinging to her deck, and those swimming around him, shouted louder than Lusitania's death groans.

He couldn't see Clyde, but his instincts kicked in. He had to swim away from the tumbling Lusitania as quickly as he could.

Chapter 27

Sixteen minutes of terror, and Lusitania was nearly gone. Martha's boat rowed away, far enough not to be sucked under water by the sinking ship. The ship didn't have much longer. In another minute or two, Martha and her boat could safely row back and pluck swimmers from the cold Irish water.

Lusitania groaned and twisted, black smoke still pouring from her funnels. Her long stern stood high in the air. People packed the stern's decks with nowhere else to go! No more boats could be lowered. Nothing to do but wait for Lusitania to slip into the sea below them.

But her motion was odd, Martha thought. The ship wasn't sinking forward. It was like the stern was settling back down while disappearing into the water. She wondered if Lusitania's bow had already hit the bottom of the shallow sea off Kinsale Head?

What an odd thought to have at a time like this, she said to herself.

Then, she prayed for Leo and Mrs. Beauclerk, that somehow, they were safe.

Somehow.

***

Mrs. Beauclerk sat on her deck chair too long. By the time she realized her own danger, it was too late. She climbed up the stairs to the boat deck, but all the boats that could be lowered had been lowered!

Yet, she remained eerily calm. She didn't panic or scream like the passengers around her. She didn't run, but calmly walked towards the stern as it climbed higher into the air.

As a lady, her shoes weren't meant for climbing the steep, wooden, wet decks. The deck grew steeper and steeper, and she slipped! She slid all the way down the wet deck and splashed into the water where the forward boat deck used to be.

And still, she stayed calm! Without even thinking about it, she kicked off her shoes and began to swim! Arm after arm, stroke after stroke, she pulled and kicked herself away from the ship, her dress fluttering in the waves behind her.

But then, somehow, she felt herself pulled back in. No matter how hard she tried, she couldn't swim away. She pulled harder and harder, and just kept getting sucked closer and closer to the ship.

Not just the ship, but the forward funnel. The top of the massive funnel had just slipped below the water, and sucked all the water around it like a whirlpool down into the ship's belly.

The whirlpool grew and sucked in chairs, bags, and anything else floating nearby... including Mrs. Beauclerk! Suddenly, the water pulled faster and faster and she was powerless against the stream as it sucked her into the funnel. In a single moment, she went from under the clear blue sky into the utter blackness of Lusitania's boilers.

And then, in another single moment, back to the blue sky! She flew through the air as if Lusitania's belly had belched her out. She kicked and thrashed and landed away from the ship with a splash. She floated to the surface and caught her breath. Even *that* wasn't enough to make her panic.

She examined herself as she floated on her back. Her dress: black. Her arms: black. Legs: black. Every inch covered with coal soot instantly baked on by her sudden adventure up and down the coal shoot.

Suddenly, two pairs of hands grabbed each of her shoulders and yanked her out of the water! Before she knew what was happening, she lay on the floor of one of the few lifeboats rowing away from the disaster.

The passengers in the boat said nothing, they just stared at her.

"She's all black, Mom!" a little girl in the back shouted, immediately shushed by her mother who tried desperately to stay polite in the middle of this complete disaster.

"Thank you," Mrs. Beauclerk told the boat, and the two crewmen who plucked her from the water. "Truly, thank you."

A loud groan sounded over the water. Lusitania's hull stretched and strained as she took her final plunge. All the boat could do was watch.

Chapter 28

Air hissed and spewed out of every opening on Lusitania's final decks above water. Only the very back still remained dry. As it settled down lower and lower all the air inside rushed out. Doors flew open, windows burst, and clouds of smoke escaped out the vents from below.

Time was up. Officer Bestic grunted and strained to help push overboard the last collapsible boat they could. His deck now hung only a few feet above the water. Quickly, he climbed the railing, and dove into the water! He jumped as hard as he could to get far, far away from the ship.

But it wasn't enough. As Lusitania's stern finally sank under water, the great suction force pulled everything around with it, including Officer Bestic. He was dragged under, like ghosts pulled at his ankles, powerless to fight against it. But fight he did. He swam up. Up, and up, and up. He swam for what he felt were miles without a breath.

But the water became lighter. He swam more, determined to make it to the surface. Finally, his head found air! But it was dark. He looked around, and saw he had surfaced under an overturned lifeboat.

He pushed his way out from under the boat and into the clear sky.

Lusitania was gone.

In her place, a thousand souls swam on the water's surface, screaming for rescue.

"Give me your hand, I'll help you up, mate!"

Bestic turned his head toward the voice. A man clinging to the top of the overturned boat offered his hand, trying to help Bestic find a spot.

He looked around. This boat would soon be swamped with people seeking refuge, just like him. He had just pushed a half dozen boats into the water in Lusitania's final moments. He had to go get one.

Off in the distance, a collapsible floated upright and empty. He pushed off this overturned boat, and swam towards his collapsible.

The water was cold. Above freezing, yes, but still cold. He hoped others were still swimming toward the empty boats he set loose.

After a few minutes of swimming, he reached the empty collapsible boat. He looked inside. Water slowly trickled through a hole in the boat's bottom.

Debris floated all around the boat. Pieces of the ship, of clothing, of baggage, of what used to be tables and chairs and dinner napkins and children's toys. He grabbed a few of the smaller pieces and threw them into the boat. Thankfully, the oars were still inside.

He reached over the boat's collapsed railing and pulled himself aboard, and quickly stuffed debris into the hole to slow the flooding as much as possible. Then, he raised the canvas sides, set the oars, and rowed back to the crowd floating where Lusitania once floated, 12 miles off Kinsale Head.

As he rowed, flocks of seagulls flew in, circling above the swimming crowd.

Not far, someone in the water waved and shouted. Bestic couldn't hear what he was shouting, but set and rowed as hard as he could toward the man. When he reached the stranded soul, he recognized him!

"Clyde!" he shouted. "Grab my hand, I'll pull you aboard!"

Clyde's cold muscles barely worked, but together, Clyde flopped himself over the boat's railing and landed on the bottom, the cold sea water dripping off his blue sailor's uniform.

He lay on the floor, catching his breath. Then, he smiled and joked with his rescuer. "I'm afraid it wouldn't do any good to ask for a towel, wouldn't it?"

Bestic smiled, and pulled a handkerchief out of his pocket. "Afraid mine's a little soggy."

Together, they shared a laugh. But then, Bestic's face turned serious, seeing the broken handcuffs still chained to Clyde's wrist. "How'd you get out?" he asked.

"Leo came and rescued me!" Clyde answered. "We escaped out a porthole once the ship was already under water!" Then, Clyde looked out over the water, at the sea of survivors in the near distance. "Suppose he made it?"

Bestic handed him an oar. "Let's go find out," he said. Then, skilled and determined sailors as they were, the two of them rowed to the crowd to save as many people as possible.

Chapter 29

Two hours ago, while setting off to fish the coast of Ireland, the small sail-powered fishing boat *Wanderer* heard rumors of Lusitania's demise. The crew of seven raised all her sails and made full speed toward Old Head of Kinsale.

But the Wanderer only had sails, and the wind was slight. Progress was slow as the tiny vessel inched across the water's surface. The frustrated crew could do nothing but wait for the gentle breeze to push them toward Kinsale Head.

Unknown to the Wanderer's crew, a small fleet of fishing boats and pleasure yachts were also slowly making their way toward Kinsale

Head. None of them had the power of Cunard or the Royal Navy, but they had sails, and they could float. Their crews determined that they would help, even if their ship was only big enough to rescue a dozen of Lusitania's survivors.

The *Wanderer*. The *City of Exeter*. The *Etonian*. The *Narragansett*. The *Flying Fish*. The *Galloping Goose*. The *Julia*. A ragtag group of fishing trawlers, yachts, and tugboats. Lusitania's rescue fleet was on its way. Each of the captains of each of the tiny ships knew they were putting their own vessels in harm's way, speeding through the same submarine-infested waters that just claimed *Lusitania*.

It would take hours, and darkness began to set. Some survivors huddled for warmth in the boats, and others clung to the sides of overturned boats and floating deck chairs. But when the steam and sails of their rescuers arrived, though they were safe, they couldn't yet breathe a sigh of relief until they knew the fates of their loved ones.

Chapter 30

The haphazard navy that rescued Lusitania's survivors began pulling into the lamp-lit harbor of Queenstown under cover of night. By morning, hotels and businesses around Queenstown posted lists of the names of survivors on their storefronts.

As day broke on May 8th, a sleepless Martha sent a telegram to her mother in Liverpool. *I am saved*, the telegram read. *Looking for Leo*. She paused for a moment and shuddered, for her mother may not have even known that either of them were aboard the Lusitania.

Dozens, if not hundreds of people gathered around Martha. She still wore her maid's outfit, and she clutched a blanket around her for warmth. The crowd of survivors, family, and simply curious onlookers read through the lists of survivors.

Quite a task it was, to assemble such a list. Each of the dozen or so ships that brought in survivors arrived at different times, and no one knew whether or not more ships were on their way. Those who didn't see their loved ones' names on the list certainly hoped more were coming.

Martha found herself surrounded by screams of joy and sobs of sorrow, and of desperate prayers by those who remained unsure. She looked up and down each list, reading closely for Leo's name.

She hadn't found it.

Mrs. Beauclerk was saved. So, too, appeared to be Captain Turner. But the name of Seaman Leo Masterson had not yet appeared on any of the lists. *Maybe there was a special list*, she thought, *just for crew?*

She reached the bottom of one list posted to the side of the hotel's brick wall, and stepped to her right to re-read the next list. With her step, she bumped into a stranger studying the list for himself.

"My apologies, I-"

She stopped, and looked at the man she bumped into. He was wearing blue.

Leo.

Leo! They saw each other at the same time, and instantly burst into joyous tears. They were safe. They were safe! It was really him. It was really her!

Leo's friend George was with him, but Leo ignored him and jumped to hug his sister. They just stood, hugging each other, a big long hug for the first time since they were little kids in their mother's yard.

"How did you survive?" Martha asked through her joyous tears.

Leo just smiled. "Remember that time I almost died?"

Martha just nodded.

"I know a lot more than I did back then."

The End.

Epilogue

1,959 passengers and crew boarded Lusitania in New York on May 1, 1915.

761 survived after Lusitania was torpedoed by the U-20 off Old Head of Kinsale, Ireland. She sank in 18 minutes.

Captain Turner survived the sinking, and was put on trial. Cunard and the British Navy claimed he was responsible for putting Lusitania in harm's way. He was found not guilty.

It would take nearly two years, but the death of over one hundred Americans aboard eventually pushed the United States to join Britain in World War One.

Notes

For this book, the characters of Leo and Martha, as well as Mrs. Beauclerk, George, and Clyde are fictional characters who did not exist. Their stories are loosely based on the experiences of several real people.

Captain Turner and Junior Third Officer Bestic were real. I didn't feel it was appropriate to invent new names for Lusitania's Captain nor her officers. Though some of their actions were fictionalized, I did my best to stay true to their intentions and motivations throughout the story, in order to honor their legacy and memory.

***

Also by David Dubczak
For young readers:

DASH: The Carpathia's Mad Race to Save the Titanic

***

The crew felt a new wind. The bitter cold added to the bite of a ship that had never, ever gone this fast. Sharp eyes stayed fixed on the dim horizon. There was no time for caution, though they knew dangerous ice lay ahead. The tiny vessel Carpathia raced into the same ice field that had just claimed Titanic.

Young Henry Cromwell dreams of becoming a reporter. Armed with a homemade radio, he spent the first three days of Carpathia's voyage secretly listening in on the North Atlantic's radio traffic—eagerly jotting down notes and being a general bother to the crew. But nothing prepared him for what he would hear at 12:30 am.

In the bitter cold air and moonless night, every crew member is awake. While the passengers slept, the Carpathia came alive, ready to take on Titanic's passengers... if they make it in time.

***

DASH Chapter 3

After dinner didn't bring an exciting adventure with Maria. Instead, Henry's mother kept him in the dining room, and insisted that he stay there and learn how to conduct himself and hold conversations in polite company. Naturally, he hated this, and resented not being allowed to leave.

What's more is he saw Maria at the other end of the dining room, and when she left, he wasn't allowed to follow! *She must be bored, too*, he thought, and fidgeted in his chair until Mother slapped his knee.

Eventually, the sun set and they retired back to their room. It was simply too cold to remain on deck any longer. Slowly, the passengers of the Carpathia, full from dinner and drowsy from the bitter Atlantic air, withdrew back to their rooms, turned out the lights, and went to sleep.

Everyone, except Henry. He wished he could sleep, as more sleep let him pass away the boredom. But Mother's snoring assured him that if he worked quietly, he could plug in his radio and have a listen, if only for a few more minutes. As he waited at the dinner table that evening, he could almost feel his fame, the Kronen, and even his father getting further away. He *needed* to listen.

Slowly and quietly, he pulled back the curtain and hooked up his antenna. It was so dark out it wouldn't matter, anyway. Next, taking quiet, slow steps, muffled by the vibration from the ship's engines, tip-toed to the light switch, and clipped on his electrical cable. Then, he tucked himself into bed, put his headset over his ears, and pushed his pillow over his head to further drown out the sound.

What he heard next utterly shocked him. Immediately, his eyes widened. He had been listening every evening for the past three days, but he had never heard this.

-.-. --.-

C Q

He knew the Marconi company's codes, and CQ was a general call signal, used when an operator had something important to say to everyone. Radio operators only used this if they had something very important to say, and they wanted everyone else to stop transmitting. What was the important thing this operator was saying?

-..

D

Distress. CQD - All Stations, Distress. He was in trouble. But who? Henry recalled his list of ships' call signs.

-- --. -.--

M G Y

CQD MGY. All Stations, Distress.

Henry shivered. This one was new. It had just come online. He had only heard it for the first time in the past few days. He needed light to double-check his list of station codes, but he was almost *certain* he was right. Seeing this ship's name on his list had already excited him, and he hoped he would hear it as they passed each other in the middle of the Atlantic.

But he certainly didn't want to hear it for the first time next to CQD - All Stations, Distress.

-- --. -.--

M G Y

Titanic.

DASH: The Carpathia's Mad Race to Save the Titanic

is available through

Amazon

Barnes and Noble

Direct from author at www.DavidDWriter.com

or ask your favorite local bookstore to order through Ingram.

About the Author

David Dubczak is an educator, author, and playwright. His interest in ships, including the Lusitania, stretches back to elementary school. Originally from Holmen, Wisconsin, he lives in Iowa with his wife Laura and dog Avila, whom they affectionately refer to as "Noodle."

You can read his plays and check out his other writings, with more to come, at DavidDWriter.com.

Look for "David Dubczak – Writer" on social media.

Like this book? Amazon and GoodReads reviews are essential to helping independent authors grow their brand. Please share how much you enjoyed this book!

www.ingramcontent.com/pod-product-compliance
Lightning Source LLC
Chambersburg PA
CBHW021809130726
47987CB00010B/3079